Bird Talk

Hilariously Accurate Ways to Identify Birds by the Sounds They Make

Written and illustrated
by Becca Rowland

Storey Publishing

For my Mum, who started this all.

The mission of Storey Publishing is to serve our customers by
publishing practical information that encourages
personal independence in harmony with the environment.

Edited by Kristen Hewitt
Art direction & book design by Ian O'Neill
Text production by Jennifer Jepson Smith

Storey Publishing
210 MASS MoCA Way
North Adams, MA 01247
storey.com

Storey Publishing is an imprint of
Workman Publishing, a division of
Hachette Book Group, Inc., 1290 Avenue
of the Americas, New York, NY 10104.
The Storey Publishing name and logo are
registered trademarks of Hachette Book
Group, Inc.

ISBNs: 978-1-63586-923-1
(paperback with flaps);
978-1-63586-957-6 (ebook)

Printed in China by Toppan Leefung
Printing Ltd. on paper from
responsible sources
10 9 8 7 6 5 4 3 2 1

TLF

Library of Congress Cataloging-in-
Publication Data on file

Contents

1

We Can't Help It If We're Popular
Some of Your Basic Birds

2

It Doesn't Mean What You Think
Birds with Suggestive Names

3

Someone Has to Play the Villain
Scavengers and Predators

4

Do You Have a Towel?
Birds That Love the Water

5

Who? I Think You Mean Whom
Let's Talk About Owls

6

Ha Ha! Fooled You Again
Birds That Sound like Other Animals

7

Not from Around These Parts
Birds Not from North America

8

Human Is as Human Does
Birds That Sound like Us

9

Come Here Often?
Birds That Travel and Those That Don't

10

Cacophony, Commotion, and Clarity
Birds with Unique Sounds

If It Sounds Like . . .

It is a truth universally acknowledged that we will all get to that stage in life where we start to notice the birds around us. Our own personal bird era, if you will, might start when we are young with a fascination with nature or with a pet bird or with a cartoon parrot from a beloved children's movie.

But for other people, and I dare say the majority, this bird era happens later in life. One day we astonish ourselves with how extremely excited we become at seeing the crimson flash of a cardinal flying by, get goose bumps when hearing the eerie tone of a loon in the early morning, or have an otherworldly moment locking eyes with an owl resting in a tree, as if seeing magic itself. It's around the same time in life when we start saying things like "Wow, it's really coming down out there" during a rainstorm, or when going to bed before ten on a weekend sounds like our idea of a really great night.

There are billions of birds in the world—more than 10,000 different species—and they are top of the list for animals we know by sound. That said, learning the particularities of their sounds is

akin to learning another language in which at best we're able to ask for directions to the train station. But when you know which bird you've just heard, you level up a little. In the same way you point out the window of a moving car and yell "Cow!" every time you see one, you may start yelling "Blue jay!" or "Raven!" as you walk through the park. Feel the power that comes from being the mysterious cool friend who can instinctively identify birds from hearing their songs.

Now, not every birdsong or call has an explainable counterpart. Songbirds, like warblers and wrens, are so melodic that they sound exactly like music. Others sing as well as that friend who thinks they are about to be plucked from the stage at karaoke night directly onto their first world tour. We've all tried to describe a tune to friends with some bad humming or off-key singing and know how excruciating that can be—hopefully the comparisons in this book can save you from that.

Birds have different calls and sounds for locations, time of day, alarms, being flirtatious, sometimes just generally being annoying, and heaps of other situations. This book won't explain each

sound or call. It will try to connect a sound you already know and can hear in your brain to one of the sounds that a bird makes.

Most nature guides these days explain bird sounds with phonetic descriptors like *kweek* or *chee-chee* or say the song has a harsh trill or a careless whisper. This way of explaining bird sounds isn't the most intuitive. Connecting the bird sounds to tangible, explainable noises, like water dripping from a leaky faucet or a phone vibrating on a table, makes them memorable and solidifies them in your brain.

So if you find yourself thinking, *That bird sounds like it's saying the word "cheeseburger,"* don't fret, you're not having a breakdown—everyone knows birds famously prefer fries.

Are you ready? Let's begin.

1

We Can't Help It If We're Popular

Some of Your Basic Birds

These birds aren't boring, even if some are called common. They are birds you've seen and heard—you would recognize them in a children's puzzle book, or maybe guess their name in a Sunday crossword. Okay, not Sunday; let's go with a Tuesday crossword, but you'll do it in pen!

If it sounds like a chain saw...

it's a great blue heron. If you are out by the water and hear the deep sounds of a chain saw revving up, it might be one of these majestic birds (they love a river, big fans of a marsh). Or it could be someone cutting down a tree—be aware of your surroundings.

If it is a great blue heron, you might want to think before complaining about the racket. These birds, found all across North America, are almost five feet tall (ask them and they'll claim it's six) with a wingspan that can be over six feet! Even with their incredible size, they weigh less than seven pounds, but their daggerlike beak is nothing to be trifled with.

If it sounds like a siren going off…

it's a **northern cardinal.** Both male and female cardinals sing. There's a mechanical element to the noise like a child's toy police car—the siren song that you hear in the trees doesn't feel very birdlike at all. Find these loud birds in eastern Canada, the US, and Mexico.

The male wears the bright red feathers and is easily spotted, especially in the winter months. The female, however, knows how to use an accent color correctly.

Everything is an emergency - if you're loud enough

If it sounds like the shutters of paparazzi cameras firing...

it's a great-tailed grackle. This sound can make you feel glamorous and famous or cause you to quickly pull down your hat and adjust your sunglasses, depending on what you're wearing that day.

Not to be confused with the boat-tailed grackle, the great-tailed has a larger tail and is less nautically inclined. The clearest way to spot the difference is that if it has distinct yellow eyes, it's an adult great-tailed grackle. The males are often seen in groups with their heads looking straight up in a haughty manner, ready for their next close-up. Find them in the southwestern US, throughout Mexico, and into Central America.

If it sounds like a sneeze...

it's a common grackle. With a considerably shorter tail than either the great- or boat-tailed versions, the common grackle can be discerned by its beautiful blue neck and bronzed body that shows hints of purple and gold in the light. These birds live across central Canada and the US, right down to the Mexican border. Huge fans of corn, they can be spotted in fields and don't give a damn about your scarecrow.

Their sneeze sounds mechanical and metallic with a clear buildup-and-release cadence. If you sneezed like that, you'd be in the waiting room at a clinic already.

If it sounds like you are being catcalled...

it's an American robin. Their short, sharp songs have clear stops and starts that give the impression they are yelling a bunch of phrases at you. You know the stuff—"Hey baby, hey mama, you look good, hey you, look out for that pothole!"

Named after the European robin due to their matchy-matchy redbreast feathers, the American version doesn't have the orange feathers on its face. Here's a fun fact: All orange-colored things used to be called red, which is probably why we refer to some people as redheads. Then this fancy fruit called an orange became popular, and people decided, "Let's call all things that are that color *orange*."

Robins are widespread across North America, and for those in the northern parts of the continent, they are a happy indicator of warmer weather on the way as they migrate north for snacks in spring. Often seen on lawns in populated areas, they are the proverbial "early bird," getting that worm and then taking a moment to yell an unsolicited compliment your way.

If it sounds like a rusty hinge...

it's a blue jay. The rusty-hinge sound is a short two-note noise like quickly opening and closing an old, corroded metal hinge. These birds are also known for their loud, metallic *jay* call and are quite the mimic—they do one hell of a hawk impression that they like to pull out at parties.

Blue jays live year-round in central and eastern North America and are easy to identify by both their striking bright blue feathers and their loud calls. You'll often hear them before you see them. Sometimes confused with the Steller's jay, who looks like a teenager going through their punk years.

If it sounds like someone snoring...

it's an American white pelican—another beautiful bird with a less-than-beautiful sound. These enormous white birds with large beaks, which they use to scoop up fish, live throughout North America near lakes and ocean coastlines. With features that remind you most of their dinosaur ancestors, they have a wingspan that can be over nine feet!

While they don't usually make a lot of noise, when the males do call, they sound like someone snoring. Loudly. Next to you. At 3:12 a.m. We do recommend earplugs before resorting to smothering.

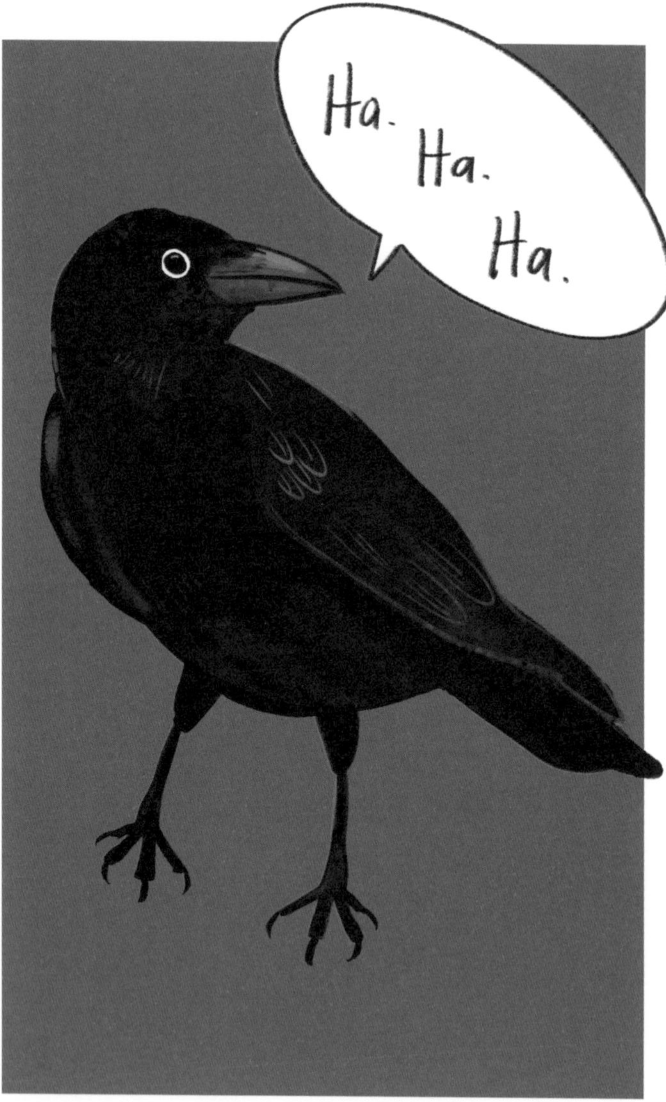
Ha. Ha. Ha.

If it sounds like someone is laughing at you...

it's an American crow. They are everywhere. Urban cities, quiet neighborhoods, open fields, in stories about witches, perched on towers and gargoyles, gathering in murders. Besides their well-known *caw caw* sound or throaty rattle noises that sound like the Predator, they can be identified by the sound of someone sarcastically laughing at you.

Clever creatures, they have been known to figure out puzzles and have a love for shiny things. They have one of the largest brain-to-body-mass ratios of all animals, right up there with dolphins and octopuses.

Crows generally tolerate humans, and some actually come to like us. It's even believed that they can remember faces. If you haven't thought about googling "how to befriend crows," maybe this book isn't for you.

If it sounds like someone disagreeing with you...

it's a fish crow. A beautiful black bird that lives mostly in Florida and along the eastern coastline of the US is the fish crow. As it is only a bit smaller than the American crow and extremely similar in appearance, they are hard to tell apart. They even hang out together just to make things more confusing. The best way to distinguish them is that if it sounds like someone is disagreeing with you, it's a fish crow.

Their *uh-uh* sound is unmistakable and slightly apathetic. They disagree with what you're saying, but they are really not that bothered and are most likely not willing to start an argument over it.

As their name suggests, they love fish and will hang out along beaches, lakes, rivers, and other waterways.

If it sounds like a phone vibrating on a table...

it's a common raven. I never understood why that *brrr brrr brrr* sound was considered less invasive than my Star Wars ringtone. And who's calling me, anyway? Don't you know about texting?

These large black birds have feathers that look like scales and appear to form armor. Known as an all-black bird, in the light their feathers illuminate with a rainbow of colors. Much more of a country bird than a city bird, ravens are beautiful in flight as they glide and swoop and spin. On the ground, you can tell them by their hopping walk.

While most bird groups are referred to as a flock, the collective nouns for ravens are an unkindness, a treachery, or a conspiracy. Which would give anyone a complex.

Common Raven vs. American Crow

Two large black birds of myth, lore, and legend often get mistaken for each other. Known for their cleverness, both show a deep understanding of their world, which is one of the reasons we are so fascinated by them.

The common raven is seen across North America, Europe, Asia, and parts of North Africa. They prefer mountains and deserts, while the crow likes the city scene. The American crow is found in Canada and the US. They have cousins on the Eurasian continent, such as the carrion crow or jackdaw.

Ravens have more of a bed head with fluffy, disheveled neck feathers. Crows are much sleeker.

bed head

sleek

VS

raven

crow

27 inches tall   20 inches tall

When in flight, the raven tail is shaped like an arrow-head, pointing away from the direction they're flying. Crow tails have a blunt-bangs look, with a sharper edge. Crows flap, while ravens also glide.

American crows sound like the classic *caw caw* noise that you learn in kindergarten when you learn a cow says *moo* or an elephant makes a muffled trumpet noise that you mimic while raising your arm.

Ravens sound like a crow, if that crow had a mouthful of gravel. It's a much more guttural noise.

Both make knocking, rattling, and blooping noises that would play nicely in the background of a sci-fi film.

Then there's the size difference. If you see a large black bird, you might question whether it's a crow or a raven. In that case it's probably a crow. If you see a large black bird and think *Dear god, what is that?!*, it's most likely a raven.

2

*It Doesn't Mean
What You Think*

Birds with Suggestive Names

As is the way with language, words evolve over time. The birds here have ended up with suggestive names, but that wasn't the original intention. Nuthatches like nuts, but none have been observed incubating any. There are several birds named tits, which relates to their diminutive size, not their teats. You see, birds don't have any.

If it sounds like a two-tone police siren...

it's a coal tit. Let's get this out of the way. The next few birds have names that may cause grown adults to giggle. If you're not going to take this book seriously, then . . . great! (You'll love it when we get to the booby.)

You know how police sirens have different tones in different countries and you pick up on that sound in films right away? The coal tit's British-esque two-tone siren call can be lower in pitch than North American police cars, and these birds are probably better at football. The football that is soccer, of course. The coal tit lives in Europe and Asia. These tiny little birds look like chickadees, their North American relatives, and are widespread throughout Europe, Ireland, the UK, Asia, and northern Africa!

If it sounds like
a US police siren ...

it's a tufted titmouse. Now, if you are in the
eastern United States and hear a police-siren-
sounding bird, that could be a tufted titmouse. Or
you're being pulled over. How fast were you going?

If you're not driving a vehicle, look for these
soft gray birds with a pointed tuft of feathers on
their heads like a little gnome hat. Their sound is a
two- or three-tone alarm call, similar to the coal tit.

In the western US, the juniper titmouse sounds
like a store alarm when the clerk has forgotten
to remove those tags from your purchase. When
you're a little bird, it's good to carry a big sound.
They are related to both the North American
chickadees and tits in the rest of the world. I don't
believe they have any mouse relations.

If it sounds like it's sending a message in Morse code...

it's a Eurasian blue tit. Now take the coal tit and give it a dye job. This jaunty blue, yellow, and white bird lives all across Europe, western Asia, Ireland, and the UK. I mean, they really get around! Locals there can find these friendly little birds in their backyard, local parks, and wooded areas.

If it sounds like they are sending a vital message about the location of enemy submarines in the English Channel, with some high notes and low notes that vary in speed, they are probably asking for you to refill the bird feeder.

If it sounds like it's saying cheese-burg-er...

it's a black-capped chickadee. This bird has numerous calls and songs. Some sound like *hey sweetie* or *Phoebe*, and when they use their own name—*chick-a-dee-dee*—the more *dees* you hear, the higher the threat. Probably not from you; they are pretty cool with humans.

There are seven different chickadee species. The black-capped can be found across Canada and the northern US. In North America they are called chickadees, but these species are referred to as tits in the rest of the world.

If it sounds like your cell phone is ringing...

it's a great tit. With their striking black stripe down the middle of their yellow bellies, these tits are larger than most of the other tits found in Europe, Ireland, and the UK. These tits hang out in gardens, and as one of the larger tits around, they use their size to bully some of the smaller birds. I really need to stop saying the word tit.

The phone-ringing sound isn't an old-school rotary phone ring—think more of a repetitive noise that's going off in a crowd where clearly the person whose phone it is does not hear the tone and never thought to change the default setting. This is the same person who will eventually answer that phone on speaker.

If it sounds like
a garden
sprinkler...

it's a long-tailed tit. What the long-tailed tit
gains in the length of its beautiful long and pointy
tail, it seems to lose on the other end by having
such a tiny beak. Found across Europe and Asia,
from Ireland to Japan, these miniature fluffy birds
prefer to spend time in groups.

The long-tailed tit has an American counterpart
called the bushtit, and neither is related to the
other tits in this book. They sound like a water
sprinkler—but I don't think they can do the dance.
They live for only two years, so we can forgive
them for not finding time for choreography.

If it sounds like a truck beeping as it backs up...

it's a red-breasted nuthatch. Nuthatches like to park themselves on tree trunks facing downward. Maybe that is why this bird's song sounds like a truck reversing. If it would just turn around, it wouldn't need that repeated *beep-beep-beep* noise to warn others it was moving. Perhaps they have a robust health and safety committee.

These little orange-breasted birds make this nasal noise from Alaska to Florida and all parts in between. They prefer forested areas—one assumes because of the abundance of trees on which to perch upside down. Watch for them bouncing around on the trunks and branches with a clear disregard for the theory of gravity.

If it sounds like someone who *thinks* they can whistle...

it's a blue-footed booby. We all know someone who just can't whistle—maybe it's even you! When they put their lips together and blow, only puffs of air and off-key sounds come out. That's our friend the blue-footed booby. Even their name is thought to come from a Spanish word for "fool" or "silly." With their slightly dazed expression and somewhat unbothered attitude around humans, it's not hard to make the connection.

They live in Mexico, Central America, and South America, and quite a few have breeding grounds in the Galápagos Islands. They do have stunning blue feet that make them entirely unique, but they are not the only booby. There are brown boobies, masked boobies, and red-footed boobies. How many times do I have to say *booby* before you stop giggling?

The Seven Kinds of Chickadees

North America has seven different chickadee species. The most widely seen and most populous is the black-capped chickadee, which spans coast to coast from Alaska to Newfoundland. Chances are if you see a bird you think is a chickadee, it's likely a black-capped. Their three-note call of *cheese-burg-er* or *hey swee-tie* is one of their adorable characteristics.

The Carolina chickadee looks so similar to the black-capped that one of them really needs to go home and change. They live in the southeastern US and have a four-note call, because they want to be special. These birds sound like they are in a stadium, chanting "Let's go, sports team!"

The chestnut-backed chickadee is more of a redhead, and they are West Coast birds that range from Alaska to California in a thin slice down the Pacific coast. These birds say *chick-a-dee* in their calls, but compared to the other chickadees, it's like you're listening back at 1.5x speed.

The boreal chickadee has a brown cap because black was so last year. They do not mind the snow and live in Canada and Alaska. They can come across like a black-capped with a cold, sounding slower and a bit stuffed up.

Mountain chickadees don't want to look like the black-capped, so they have a white racing stripe on their heads. But they can't get away from copying the popular bird, so they do sound remarkably similar. I'm sure they have

words about that. They like the West Coast and, shocking no one, mountainous regions.

Mexican chickadees live in, do I need to tell you? They like it warm and are the southernmost of the set. They sound more electronic, like a fax machine or dial-up internet.

The northernmost is the gray-headed chickadee, the rarest of the lot. You are not going to run into this bird. They live in Alaska and are introverts to the extreme.

3

Someone Has to Play the Villain

Scavengers and Predators

Everything needs to eat, from the most microscopic bacteria to the top of the food chain. Some of these birds are the apex predators of their own chains and only fight each other, the elements, or us. The scavengers of the bird world—like buzzards, condors, and vultures—clean up the mess found in the elements, made by each other (and us).

If it sounds like a squeaky whiteboard...

it's an American kestrel. Ever use the wrong marker on a whiteboard? Remember that moment when you're trying very hard to erase a permanent mark and applying too much pressure with the eraser while scrubbing back and forth to no avail? If a bird call sounds high-pitched, fast-paced, and squeaky just like that, it's an American kestrel.

For birds of prey, they are tiny birds, about the size of a pigeon but considerably better at hunting, and terrifically worse at delivering messages. They are well named, as you can find them throughout North, Central, and South America.

If it sounds like you've bent over and loudly ripped your pants...

it's a turkey vulture. If it is your pants, you may want to die from embarrassment. If you hear that noise and are in North or South America and are for some ungodly reason near some recently deceased animals, it's probably an angry turkey vulture who thinks you are after their next meal. That hissing noise is the warning it's intended to be, and you should leave.

With their six-foot wingspan and slightly scraggly feathers, they really lean into their villain aesthetic but are decent parents, with both partners incubating the eggs and feeding the young.

If it sounds like a dog trying to hold back a woof...

it's a black vulture. Now, a black vulture may sound less terrifying than a turkey vulture, but they are just as fierce. Black vultures vocalize like a well-trained dog who's been told not to bark at the delivery person, so they are holding in that noise—that muffled woof under their breath.

Not as widespread as their turkey cousin, they live along the east coast of the US and into the southern states, and down into Mexico and Central and South America. Smaller and all black, these vultures would look right at home in any horror or supernatural film. And for the soundtrack of that film, the young black vulture hiss would be perfect casting for the demon. There are few bird sounds that make your blood run cold, but that'll do it.

If it sounds like
a machine gun...

it's a shoebill. In my opinion, these are the most unique, unusual, and frankly made-up-looking birds. Staring at a shoebill, you fully understand how people thought the duck-billed platypus was a hoax. Standing around four feet tall, with a seven-foot wingspan, the shoebill has a massive bill that, when clapped together, sounds unnervingly like a machine gun. That *rat-a-tat-tat* is so convincing that it makes these birds even more unreal.

Their name clearly comes from the fact that their beak resembles a wooden clog of sorts. They reside in eastern Africa and mostly near water, as fish is their favorite dish. Neither a stork nor a pelican, though you can see the connection to both, they are very much their own.

Not at the top of their food chain—they live near leopards and crocodiles, for goodness' sake—they do sound terribly scary, but probably more to humans than to hyenas.

If it sounds like a donkey crossed with a demon...

it's a little penguin. This penguin is the smallest of all penguins at just over a foot tall and weighing only a few pounds. They live in Australia and New Zealand and are also known as the blue or little blue penguin and, my favorite, the fairy penguin. You can practically see the pixie dust. They swim in the sea, feeding during the day, and return to nest and sleep on land at night.

These fairylike penguins have a surprisingly hoarse and raspy call like a donkey crossed with a demon. And that demon is in a foul mood. While there are quite a few birds whose sound doesn't match their vibe (I'm looking at you, barn owl), this one might be the most disturbing contrast.

These birds have to fend off a variety of predators, from snakes and stoats to seals and sharks, and they make up for their stature with their ferocious snarl. While a peregrine falcon might pose a greater threat to a rabbit or mouse, its squeaky gull sound won't send you running. But the noise that comes out of this penguin? You'd set a personal record for a mile run.

If it sounds like the majestic scream of a bald eagle in a beer commercial...

it's a red-tailed hawk. I can feel you already starting to question this, and you can google it; I'll wait. At some point in history, it was decided that the national bird of the United States of America didn't sound regal enough, and so the red-tailed hawk was hired to do the voice-over. Maybe it's a ghostwriter? Ghost singer?

It's a shame that the magnificent red-tailed hawk doesn't get its dues, because that is one hell of a raptor. With chocolate brown and bronzed feathers, this hawk with the golden eyes is the most common hawk you'll see throughout all of North America from Alaska to the Panama Canal.

If it sounds like sneakers squeaking on a gym floor...

it's a bald eagle. Now that you know what a bald eagle does *not* sound like, the question arises, *What DOES it resemble?* Bald eagles can sound like gulls at the beach, but more often they sound like people playing basketball on a shiny new gym floor: those short, sharp, sneaker-squeak sounds as players move about the court.

And while that may not be the Hollywood eagle sound we've all come to know and love, these large birds should be loved for themselves, don't you think? You can find these beauties all over North America, usually wherever there's fish to be eaten.

Birds of Prey

You know them, you love them, you're rightfully scared of them. Birds of prey are known for their majestic size, unmatched hunting ability, hooked beaks, keen eyesight, and large, sharp talons. The saying "has the eyes of a hawk" didn't come into use by chance. You see them on currency, on flags, and definitely as mascots of sports teams and universities. We're talking eagles, hawks, falcons, ospreys, vultures, condors, and more.

The apex predator of the skies, these raptors are 100 percent carnivores, and they don't care who knows it. That hooked beak? Yeah, that's got one purpose, and it's for tearing into flesh. Those talons? Also, I mean, mostly just for tearing into flesh. There is a theme here. Look at vultures: They don't have feathers on their faces and necks because it's too messy when they eat. Seriously, these birds don't go near a vegetable.

The word *raptor* might make you first think of a large lizardlike dinosaur stalking two children in a kitchen, but the movies steered us wrong. Films have us believing that we know what a velociraptor is, but in reality those dinosaurs were feathered and about the size of a turkey. But whether it is film-accurate or just looks cool as a full-chest tattoo, your favorite bird of prey is a living dinosaur and should be revered as such. Did we mention the flesh-tearing? Reverence from a great distance is recommended.

hooked
beak

vulture

eagle

dinosaur skull

falcon

owl

4

Do You Have a Towel?
Birds That Love the Water

Some birds spend their whole lives by or on water, from wading birds on beaches to ducks on a pond to, famously, the albatross who chooses to live most of its life at sea. Mind you, not in flight the whole time—birds can float. Other birds prefer their water in an auditory manner, making calls that sound like water dripping in an elaborate ruse to fool their friends into thinking they've left the faucet on.

If it sounds like dragging a stick along a wooden fence…

it's a double-crested cormorant. Picture it: You're a small child, or maybe you're a large adult trying to find a wee bit of joy in your day—I'm not judging—and you grab a stick from the ground and drag it down a wooden fence. Can you imagine that hollow thunking sound? That's the sound of a double-crested cormorant. Their guttural, croaky noises leave no room for mistaking their lineage from dinosaurs to birds.

Often seen drying themselves with their wings wide-open in a stance suggestive of a gargoyle on a cathedral, these blue-eyed birds can be found throughout North America in areas near water, because they almost exclusively eat fish that they catch with their precision diving maneuvers. Even their beak has a slightly hooked end, perfect for fishing.

If it sounds like a leaking kitchen faucet dripping in the sink...

it's a magpie lark. You've just settled down with a nice cup of tea and your current book, or your quiet activity of choice—naps are good—when suddenly you hear the kitchen faucet drip-drip-dripping into the metal sink. Now, if you happen to be in Australia and there's a small black-and-white bird near your backyard, it could be a magpie lark.

These birds are known by a couple of different names, like mudlark, wee magpie, peewee, or Steve. Fun fact: They are neither a magpie nor a lark! They do resemble the Australian magpie with their coloring, and humans can be rather lazy when naming things, so magpie lark they became.

If it sounds like water dripping into a swimming pool...

it's a brown-headed cowbird. If a magpie lark sounds like your kitchen faucet that the landlord swears they'll fix, the brown-headed cowbird sounds like water dripping into a pool. Or a pond, or maybe still your sink, but this time it's clogged and full of water and you really need to find a new place.

The best way to tell the cowbird apart from the magpie lark is this: Are you in Australia? The cowbird lives in Canada, Mexico, and the US, so that will help narrow things down a bit.

And maybe check under the sink for a leak in either case.

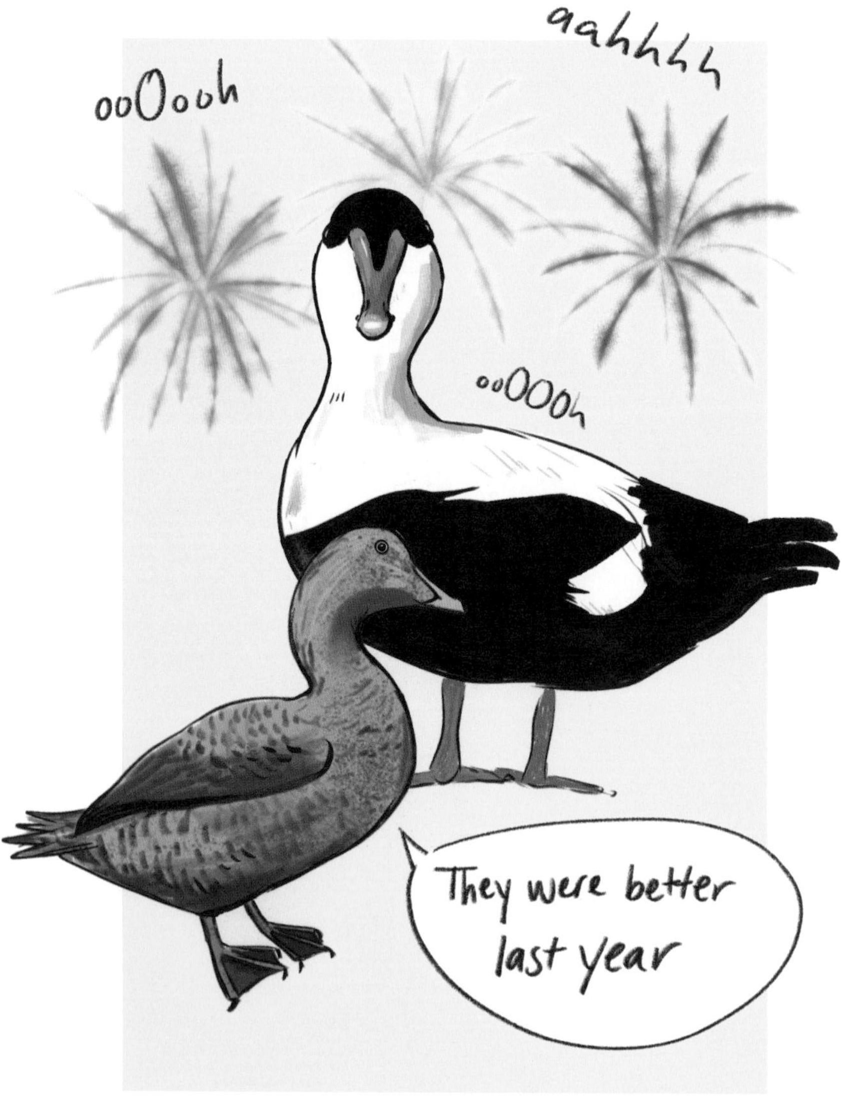
aahhhh
ooOooh
ooOOOh
They were better last year

If it sounds like someone enjoying a fireworks display...

it's a common eider. The common eider are sea ducks that know how to make a quality duvet. Humans have been collecting their down for centuries, harvested from nests when the birds are done using them. Eiderdown is revered for its softness, which matches perfectly with the quiet *oohs* and *ahs* eider ducks make. Soft feathers for a soft-sounding bird. Both their down and their sound are cushioned and cozy. Note that it's the male ducks that make this gentle cooing sound of delight and surprise. The females sound more like a frog trying to imitate a cat's purr.

Find them along the northern coastline of Canada and western Europe and down much of the eastern coast of the US in winter.

If it sounds like someone exclaiming "oooOoooh!" after hearing some juicy gossip...

it's a wedge-tailed shearwater. Spending most of their lives at sea, and ever so smartly in warm tropical waters, the wedge-tailed shearwater is a graceful flier that lives in flocks, sometimes with hundreds of birds in one grouping. Clearly a social bird, they make a call reminiscent of someone who has just been told the most scandalous news. With a rising and falling drawn-out *oooOoo*, they sound both intrigued and delighted.

Did you hear about the dentist and the golf pro? *OooOooooOoooooooo*. But have you heard what they are saying about my cousin's husband's dog walker? *OoooOOooOOoooooooo*.

Now that's good tea.

If it sounds like a clown honking their horn...

it's a trumpeter swan. I know what you're thinking: The stunning white trumpeter swan with the black bill and face calls out exactly like a trumpet, yes? Well, it's my duty to tell you that trumpeter swans sound exactly like the honking of a clown horn. Not the *a-oo-gah* noise but the two-tone *huh-huh*.

Of course you could make that noise with a trumpet, but since you can also play Miles Davis and Chet Baker songs on it, why bother mimicking a clown?

The trumpeter swan lives in pockets in Canada and the US on large bodies of water. It needs the large expanse of water to get up to speed for flight, being one of the largest and heaviest flying birds in North America. You would need a good run-up if you were trying to get 25 pounds airborne, too.

If it sounds like you are using the windshield wipers on your car but it isn't raining hard enough...

it's a weka. The raindrops are bothering you, so you swish them away, but since it's not that wet out, the wipers make that dry squeaky sound as they drag across the window. That's a weka noise!

The weka is a flightless rail native to New Zealand and found only in that country. They are a little under two feet tall—about the size of an average chicken. This makes them much larger than other rails, like the yellow rail in North America at less than half that. Size isn't everything, though.

If it sounds like a DJ scratching records...

it's a ruddy turnstone. With a name like an old-fashioned British put-down for a snitch— "How dare you, you ruddy turnstone!"—this wading, speckled bird prefers a rocky beach along the coastline of North America, hatching eggs way up in the arctic north of Canada. Happiest on a beach but not so much in the water, they like long walks on the shoreline with their head down, looking in all the tiny tide pools and flipping over rocks in search of insects and shells.

They can sound like laser tag guns firing, but their longer song is very reminiscent of a '90s DJ who got their first set of turntables and has just learned how to scratch records—a sound that always reminds me of playing with my winter parka zipper as a child.

If it sounds like someone clicking a pen...

it's a green kingfisher. Living in Texas, Mexico, and Central and South America, this brightly colored bird has a long, sharp beak that looks a bit too big for its face. They use their beaks for fishing (they are pescatarians) and thus are almost always found near water.

They sound like that one person in a meeting who's clicking a pen over and over and over again while you're trying to give your presentation, only now you can't focus on your own notes and you're stumbling over your words because they Won't. Stop. Clicking!

Where was I? Right, birds.

If you think it looks like a kookaburra, you're not wrong. Kookaburras are the largest of all the kingfishers. (See page 177.)

If it sounds like a muffled trombone...

it's a brant. This brown-and-black goose with a small white patch on the neck is also called a brent, both of which derive from the word *burnt*, reflecting their black head and neck, as if they were standing a wee bit too close to the fire. They prefer the cold and live in the Arctic along the coast of Canada, Greenland, Iceland, and parts of Europe, but they winter in warmer locales because January in the Arctic Circle is a bit harsh for anyone.

They sound like Charlie Brown's teacher with a muffled, guttural, trombonelike call that breaks apart like words in a sentence. I used to think that the cartoon adults spoke that way because the children found what they were saying inconsequential and boring, but the kids always answered and seemed to understand, so I guess it's up to us to imagine what they were saying. Goes the same for the geese—you get to write your own dialogue.

If it sounds like a metronome...

it's a northern shoveler. The northern shoveler is well spotted with its flat, spoonlike bill and by the metronomic *tick-tick* sound it makes. That said, a metronome is perfectly timed, whereas the shoveler duck has slightly more of a heartbeat sound, the sound in a scary film when it's all gone quiet and you only hear a heartbeat pounding. Or that heartbeat from under your floorboards that keeps getting louder and louder, it just won't stop beating, it's all you can hear, all you can focus on, surely others are hearing it, too!

Or, you know, a metronome.

Northern shovelers live in North America from Alaska to Mexico, migrating for breeding and food. And like other ducks, they hang out in wetlands and marshes.

Nest Sweet Nest

Nests, we all have them. Oh wait, no, that's not true.
Nests, every bird has one. Uh, also not accurate.
Nests, some birds have them.

cup nest

When you picture a bird's nest, you probably imagine something small, round, made of tiny twigs with a few blue or white speckled eggs inside, located in a tree. Many nests do have this cup shape, like an American robin's nest, but bird nests come in a vast array of sizes, shapes, and materials, like that of the ovenbird, which gets its name from the clay oven–like nest that it builds.

ovenbird nest

Some birds use cavities in the earth or plants to make cavelike nests. Woodpeckers employ their unique beaks to make large holes in trees to house their babies, and some owls take over burrows from other animals to house their young.

cavity nest

Large birds like herons and eagles build flat slab platforms very high up for their nests and then seem pretty cool about allowing us to pop a livestreaming webcam on it.

Many penguins breed in rookeries, and their nests are made from tiny rocks and pebbles. King and emperor penguin parents take turns holding their eggs on their little feet and forgo the nest altogether.

Common eiders line their nests with their own luxurious feathers to protect the eggs, and we later collect those feathers for our coats and blankets. Other water-birds construct tiny floating rafts for their nests, keeping them safe and mobile.

Not every bird is into a DIY project—some prefer a less arduous route. Plovers scratch out an area on rocky beaches to hold their eggs, which, with their coloring, is still an effective camouflage, if less likely to get them featured in *Architectural Digest*.

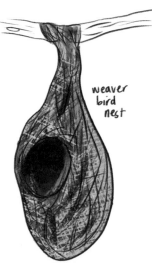

weaver bird nest

One of the most elaborate and heavily engineered nests belongs to the weaver bird. These gorgeous birds are named well for their intricately woven nests. The nest is made by the male before a couple has declared their situationship; apparently the better the nest, the more likely one is to get a date.

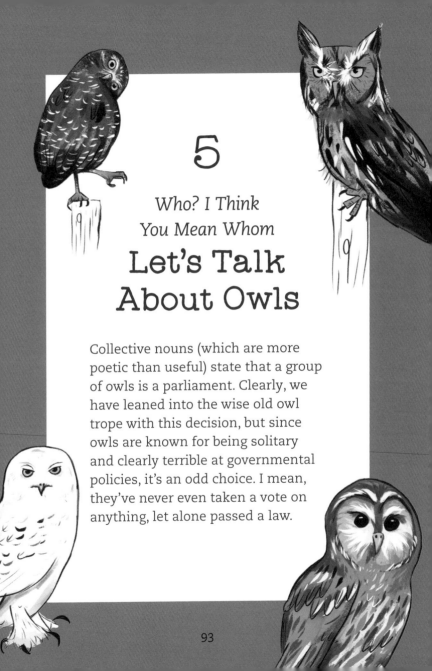

5

Who? I Think You Mean Whom

Let's Talk About Owls

Collective nouns (which are more poetic than useful) state that a group of owls is a parliament. Clearly, we have leaned into the wise old owl trope with this decision, but since owls are known for being solitary and clearly terrible at governmental policies, it's an odd choice. I mean, they've never even taken a vote on anything, let alone passed a law.

If it sounds like someone absolutely SCREAMING...

it's a barn owl. I don't mean yelling. I don't mean wailing. I don't mean the surprised yelp you make when your toast pops up a little too aggressively. I mean a person standing three feet behind you and letting loose a primal scream from the depths of their soul with all their might and fury. These nocturnal birds make sure you hear this blood-curdling scream at night because they're jerks. Beautiful, ethereal jerks.

Find them on every continent except Antarctica.

You okay, buddy?

If it sounds like someone shivering...

it's a tawny owl. The tawny owl lives in Europe and, like the barking owl (page 121), is well dressed for life among the trees. The tawny owl song suggests they might be feeling a bit chilly outside hiding in the forest, with the sound you make if you had a particularly violent cold shiver. Maybe your friend just put an ice cube down the neck of your shirt simply to watch you wriggle.

The tawny owl is also well known for duets, the classic *twit-twoo* back-and-forth calls as if they were playing a game of Marco Polo in the trees.

If it sounds like a kettle whistling...

it's a snowy owl. Don't tell the other owls, but I think the snowy owl is the most beautiful: their snow-white feathers dotted with dark brown spots, their fluffy feet obscuring those massive talons, their incredible eyes. Found across most northern and Arctic tundra regions, these owls are quite large at around two feet tall.

One of the sounds they make is akin to a kettle whistling when it's on the boil. An easy way to remember that these gorgeous birds are one of the few owls out in the daytime is that they have the kettle on for afternoon tea.

If it sounds like someone playing a kazoo...

it's a long-eared owl. Looking like the more well-known great horned owl is the long-eared owl, found in forests in North America and Europe. With their signature long, tufted ears, their coloring makes them incredibly hard to find among the branches. Add to that their nocturnal nature, and you'll be hard pressed to see one.

To hear the female owl, though, listen for someone humming on a kazoo. It's a remarkably similar sound and would be out of place as you walk through the woods at night. It's hard to think of the sound of a kazoo not being out of place unless it's the 1920s and you're in a jazz band.

The male long-eared owl makes a hoot rather like the noise you'd get from a toddler if you asked them what sound an owl makes. The male owls went classic with their noise, after all the looks and giggles the female owls were getting.

If it sounds like you're trying to get into a bath that's too hot…

it's an African wood owl. The African wood owl, with its large, black, soulless eyes, could seem a bit sinister, until you hear that one of the sounds they make is the cry you'd utter when stepping into a bathtub where the water was hotter than expected. Because you didn't test it—you were too excited, weren't you? You know when you run a tub with bubbles and you light candles and start to get in and it's right on the edge of being too hot but not hot enough to get out? Those *Oh! WooOoho! Oo!* noises you make? That's an African wood owl.

They live throughout sub-Saharan Africa all the way south to Cape Town, and as their name suggests, they prefer woodlands and forests and come out after the lights go down.

If it sounds like someone winning big at the casino…

it's a burrowing owl. The burrowing owl has such an expressive face, it would be rubbish at playing poker. These little cuties don't like forests and prefer open grasslands and deserts in North and South America, where they live in burrows underground as if they saw a prairie dog once and thought, *Oh yeah, that's the life for me!*

While they may not be able to hide their expressions long enough to win a round of cards, one of their songs sounds like they've just hit the jackpot on the slot machine. You can almost picture them raising both their little wings, thrusting them into the air with a triumphant "WOO-HOO!"

If it sounds like someone asking "Who cooks for you?"…

it's a barred owl. One of the larger owl species, the barred owl hides impeccably well within the trees that it lives around. The first time I saw one I only noticed it because it flew from one tree to another, and when your eye catches something with a three-foot wingspan flying near you in perfect silence, it really kicks in your fight-or-flight response.

They live in Canada and the US and more precisely in my backyard. They're famously known for their two-part call of *Who cooks for you? Who cooks for you allllll?*

And out of politeness I always yell back, "It's takeout!"

If it sounds like someone learning to play a recorder...

it's a northern saw-whet owl. Opposite in size to the barred owl are these precious little ones. Adding to their overall cuteness is that they sound like a child playing the recorder for the first time. Little hollow *toot-toot-toot* sounds. I know what you are thinking, but you can't have one as a pet. (I checked!)

They live in Canada, Mexico and the US and are the only bird that will fully trigger your cute aggression.

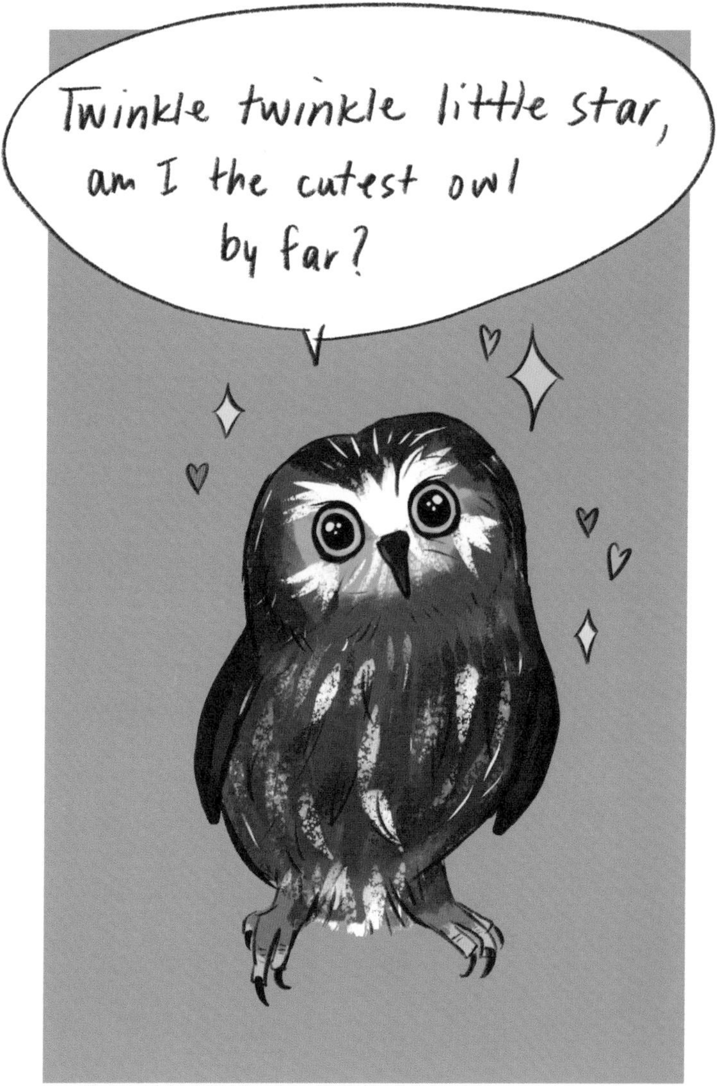
Twinkle twinkle little star, am I the cutest owl by far?

If it sounds like
a bouncing ball...

it's a western screech owl. I don't know
who named this owl, but it most certainly does
not screech. In fact, the female sounds like you've
dropped a ping-pong ball that is bouncing quickly
away from you. With feathers designed to look
like the bark of the tree it's sitting in, these owls
live in the West of North America. If you drew a
line straight down from the southeast corner of
British Columbia to the Texas panhandle, you
could have western screech owls on the left and
eastern screech owls on the right. While they look
very similar, they are not the same bird and have
a real oil vs. water thing going on. They do not mix.

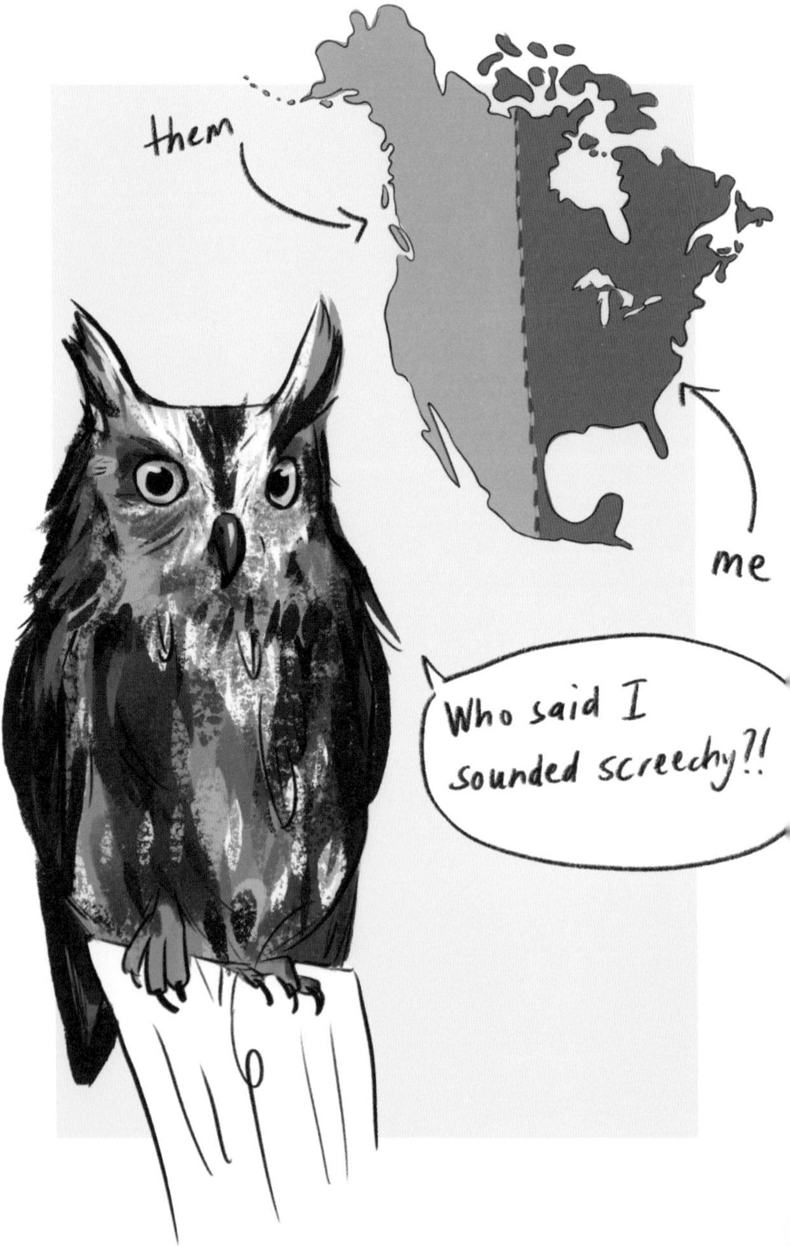
them
me
Who said I sounded screechy?!

If it sounds like
a horse neighing...

it's an eastern screech owl. If you think that those on the West Coast are not great at naming owls, the East Coast would like a word with you. The eastern screech owl is also not a screecher! It does sound exactly like the whinny of a horse. Which is an odd sound to hear coming from 10 feet over your head in a tree, let me tell you.

When these two were getting named, the barn owl must have been livid, as that owl truly lives up to the moniker of "one who screeches." Instead, the barn owl got named for that one place they lived that one time.

Owls: Not Just for Fantasy Novels

Of all the thousands of birds that have lived in the world, owls are pretty unique. We have immortalized them in literature, song, fables, and lollipop commercials. They are raptors and brutally efficient killing machines but still are seen as wise, gentle, and magical.

Ranging in size from the tiniest elf owl, who would fit in the palm of your hand, to the enormous Blakiston's fish owl, who weighs 10 pounds, they can be found all over the globe on every continent except Antarctica and live in numerous habitats and manners.

One of the most famous owl characteristics is their ability to move their heads in seemingly impossible ways. Since owls can't move their eyes within their heads, which you are probably doing just by reading this, they have to be able to move their entire head. Try holding your eyes still and fixed and then look around where you are—you'd want the most range of motion you could get, too.

Most owls are nocturnal, which adds to their mysterious aura, and can fly almost perfectly silently, which is both terrifying and impressive. Some eat insects, fish, small rodents (sometimes whole), and some eat other owls. Barred owls will leave a territory if great horned owls move in, out of fear for their lives.

great
gray
owl

barn
owl

burrowing
owl

Beautifully camouflaged in their respective habitats, owls use sound to communicate, but more so are some of the best listeners of all the animals. Their face shape is often concave, and with their ear placement this allows them to pinpoint the smallest noise from incredible distances. So if you are a mouse trying to hide under the snow, or if you are talking about someone behind their back, you might want to hush up.

talons

6

Ha Ha! Fooled You Again

Birds That Sound like Other Animals

Does a bird that sounds like a cat sound as sweet? Not all birds are melodic songbirds serenading us with their music as they fetch our ribbons and thread in the fairytale that we very much do not live in. A few birds, however, do incredible impressions of other animals with their songs and calls. What is their endgame? Are they taking their show on the road? Are they luring us into the woods hoping we have kibble? Maybe keep some in your pocket, just in case.

If it sounds like a donkey braying...

it's an African penguin. The classic tuxedo-wearing black-and-white penguin is nicknamed the jackass penguin. No, that's not because it's a jerk that borrows your car and returns it with an empty gas tank and a new dent; it's because it makes the *hee-haw* of a donkey. These penguins live around the coast of South Africa and Namibia, with a popular colony near Cape Town that you can visit. They can be hospitable hosts, but remember to bring a gift—a bouquet of fish goes over quite well. The little pink patch over the eye is actually bare skin and helps them cool down in the warmer climate. Or maybe it just looks good.

If it sounds like a dog barking...

it's a barking owl. The perfectly named—you know where I'm going with this—barking owl makes a sound like a dog saying *woof woof* in that classic two-note dog bark. (Seriously, who names these?) This Australian nocturnal owl with the expressive face and gigantic yellow eyes probably takes much pleasure from taunting the neighborhood dogs.

Its mottled coloring makes for excellent camouflage in forests and wooded areas. So before you yell at your neighbor that their dog is barking again—check the trees.

If it sounds like tossing a rock into a pond…

it's an American bittern. That delightful *plunk* noise. You know you can't resist tossing a large rock into some water when you get the chance— we can't all be good at skipping stones, can we? It's a fitting sound, for this little brown bird is found in wetlands and marshes in North America.

They can also make a call that sounds like a dog barking. Ponds and dogs, what's not to love? But whoever stole the bittern's neck, can you give it back?

If it sounds like a yowling cat...

it's a green catbird. Sometimes the names for birds don't appear to match their sound, mannerisms, or looks. The green catbird is here to dispute that. A green bird that sounds like a cat? Do I have a name for you!

This catbird lives in eastern Australia, where their green feathers help them blend into the rain forests where they like to live. Their song isn't as much like a cat meowing as a cat yelling in pain— a noise that I'm sure has fooled more than one person and had them out in the trees looking for a lost kitty who needs help.

The spotted catbird, which has similar green coloring and also makes the song of a cat yowling, lives in northern Australia and doesn't cross habitats with the green catbird. Though the green catbird is a bit spotted, too, so maybe there are no perfectly named birds? We need to be more creative with these things.

If it sounds like a whimpering dog...

it's a Canada jay. This beauty of a bird has gray and white feathers that are so soft and blended into each other, they look like they've been airbrushed. The national bird of Canada, it is also known as the gray jay and lives throughout Canada, mostly in forested areas.

They make a whistle that sounds like a dog whining and have been caught mimicking the rusty-hinge noise of a blue jay to confuse predators. Even when you are the national bird of a whole country, you still have to compete with your more popular friend. Canada jays also have been witnessed copying the sounds of other larger birds in an attempt to confuse and scare them away.

If it sounds like a newborn kitten...

it's a little owl. The little owl looks like the burrowing owl (page 104), but you won't get them confused, as the burrowing owl occurs in North America while this one lives in the UK, Europe, Asia, and North Africa. The little owl is, in fact, rather little, standing about three apples tall, and I think it is one of the birds who does the very best cat imitation. One of the calls they make sounds exactly like tiny kittens mewing.

Not sure about the benefit of sounding like a small kitten up a tree unless their endgame is to catch kindhearted people who would climb a tree to rescue a kitten. They normally eat insects and small mammals, so it seems unlikely they want us as a meal. Maybe they just want a cuddle.

If it sounds like a dog growling and barking...

it's a Canada goose. These large waterfowl are found everywhere in their namesake Canada and throughout the US and parts of western Europe. Since grass is on their menu, you can spot them on golf courses and in parks, backyards, and other places with manicured lawns. They can also sound like someone walking across a pile of rubber chickens or hiss like cats. If you hear the hissing, it's probably too late. We will speak kindly of you.

Canada geese mate for life and are ferocious in protecting their young—ask anyone who's come too close! While they're thought to have teeth on their tongue, of all places (including in your nightmares), their tongues actually have serrated side edges for gripping and tearing vegetation. That isn't making it sound less scary, though, is it?

They can be seen in the stereotypical V formation when flying overhead. There is a reason that one side of that V formation is always longer than the other— it's because it has more birds in it.

If it sounds like a cat meowing…

it's a gray catbird. Do you live in North America, and did you read earlier about the green and spotted catbird and think, *That's not fair! I want to be bamboozled by a bird pretending to be a cat!?* The gray catbird obliges. Given their gray coloring and tendency to be near the ground in woodlands, you'll hear them well before you see them.

Some of their sounds can be very droidlike and mechanical, and then *bam!* Perfect cat noise. So many people have been tricked by these sounds that it's easy to see how these birds are related to the mockingbird.

I can't tell if they are laughing at us or are utterly dismissive that we are even there.

Your Bird Zodiac

Each of the zodiac signs has different personality types and attributes. These are the birds whose characteristics match the signs the closest. Feel free to get a tattoo of your zodiac bird based on these comparisons. Or, you know, just generally—bird tattoos are cool.

Aries

Your sign is independent, feisty, energetic, and courageous. You have no filter and get bored easily. You are the fiery red and siren-sounding northern cardinal.

Taurus

Tenacious, passionate, and grounded in nature, you are patient and don't particularly like change but love a bit of glamour. You are a ruby-throated hummingbird—why fly when you can hover?

Gemini

You are outgoing, gentle, and charming. Known to start an argument just to flirt, you are communicative and curious just like your bird—the clever common raven.

Cancer

You are loyal and sentimental. You provide a feeling of home to friends and family and are quite the protector. You are a snow goose, who travels great distances in large flocks that take care of each other.

Leo

Leo the lion! You are confident, fun, charismatic, and unforgettable. You can be a bit bossy and don't mind taking charge. You are the scarlet macaw, both beautiful and sassy.

Virgo

You are clever, love a routine, and are a perfectionist. You have high standards for yourself and others. You are a king penguin who will find your mate the most perfect of pebbles to show your love.

Libra

You are cool, magnetic, and romantic—
a balanced person who doesn't like
being alone. You are a flamingo,
stunning, soft, and utterly beguiling.

Scorpio

While you are passionate, brave,
resourceful, and mysterious, you
can also be seduced by power and
control. You are a golden eagle that
soars the skies.

Sagittarius

Known to be spontaneous, defiant,
energetic, and bold, the Sag is a
born adventurer. You are a pileated
woodpecker, full of color, noise, and
showmanship.

Capricorn

Ambitious, consistent, fearless, and disciplined, you strive for great heights and almost always reach them. You are an osprey—you love to soar and look damn good doing it.

Aquarius

While you are philosophical, selfless, and intellectual, you can also be aloof and unpredictable. Your bird is the toco toucan, who is often found in contemplation with a friend hanging out in the trees.

Pisces

The romantic, who is creative, faithful, and sensitive: The sign of the fish means a bird who loves the water and who mates for life. You are a mute swan.

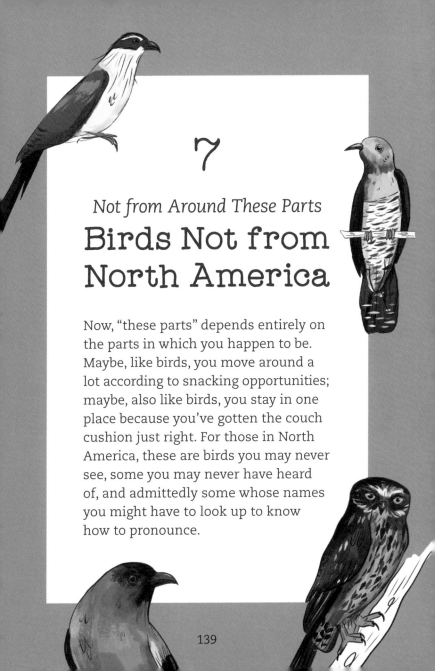

7

Not from Around These Parts
Birds Not from North America

Now, "these parts" depends entirely on the parts in which you happen to be. Maybe, like birds, you move around a lot according to snacking opportunities; maybe, also like birds, you stay in one place because you've gotten the couch cushion just right. For those in North America, these are birds you may never see, some you may never have heard of, and admittedly some whose names you might have to look up to know how to pronounce.

If it sounds like a lifeguard whistle...

it's a Cape sparrow. With its high-contrast black-and-white markings, the Cape sparrow can be recognized and remembered by the large white C on its head. C for Cape. Or cute. Or cantankerous. You'll find your own mnemonic.

Listen for the sharp blow of a lifeguard whistle, but only if you're currently in South Africa, Namibia, Botswana, and generally southern Africa. If you hear that noise in countries other than that and are by a large body of water, you're in danger of swimming into a riptide, there's a shark near you, or you're running by the pool. It says no running, Kevin!

If it sounds like a creaky old iron gate...

it's a **North Island kōkako.** These gorgeous birds are found only in New Zealand. They are blue-gray with a defined blue pouch, or wattle, under their beak. They are more likely to be heard than seen, due to their ability to blend into the trees and their low population numbers.

They make one of the most eerie sounds of any bird, the perfect backing track to a horror film. It sounds like old, rusted metal gates moving slowly in the wind in the dead of night, creaking and groaning and hauntingly beautiful.

If it sounds exactly like a cuckoo clock…

it's a common cuckoo. We all know what a cuckoo clock sounds like, either from a cartoon or your grandma having one in the hall that you would patiently sit by and wait for the hour just to watch that little birdie pop out. For some reason, it's still a bit surprising that the common cuckoo bird sounds *exactly* like that, yet there it is. If birds could sue, there would be copyright infringement.

These lovely gray birds with their stripy chests live in Europe and parts of Asia and migrate to the African continent for warmer winters and a bite to eat.

At the bottom of the list for parents of the year, cuckoos drop off their eggs in the nests of other birds for them to incubate and raise. Then the babies turn out a bit narcissistic by hatching early and taking all the food from their adopted parents. You know, let's not tell them about the clock sounds. They would really milk that lawsuit for all it's worth.

If it sounds like removing a cork from a bottle...

it's a gang-gang cockatoo. More specifically, it's the sound of straining to remove a stuck cork from a bottle after a particularly trying day and you are really not in the mood for one more thing to go wrong.

These bright-redheaded cockatoos are Australian, but you can't hear that in their accent. Known to their friends simply as gang-gang, they call southeastern Australia home. They can live up to 50 years and mate for life—which means they probably start running out of things to talk about around year 23.

If it sounds like it would like some "more pork"...

it's a morepork owl. Also known by their Māori name of ruru, these New Zealand natives are found on both the North and South Islands and are the only remaining native owls in the country. The barn owl has migrated over from Australia and started pushing into morepork territory. (As the most widespread owl in the world, the barn owl is apparently on a mission to take over the planet.)

The two-tone *more pork* call does feel a bit disconnected, since these owls mostly eat insects. Maybe they are asking for more Björk? Her albums from the '90s are quite good.

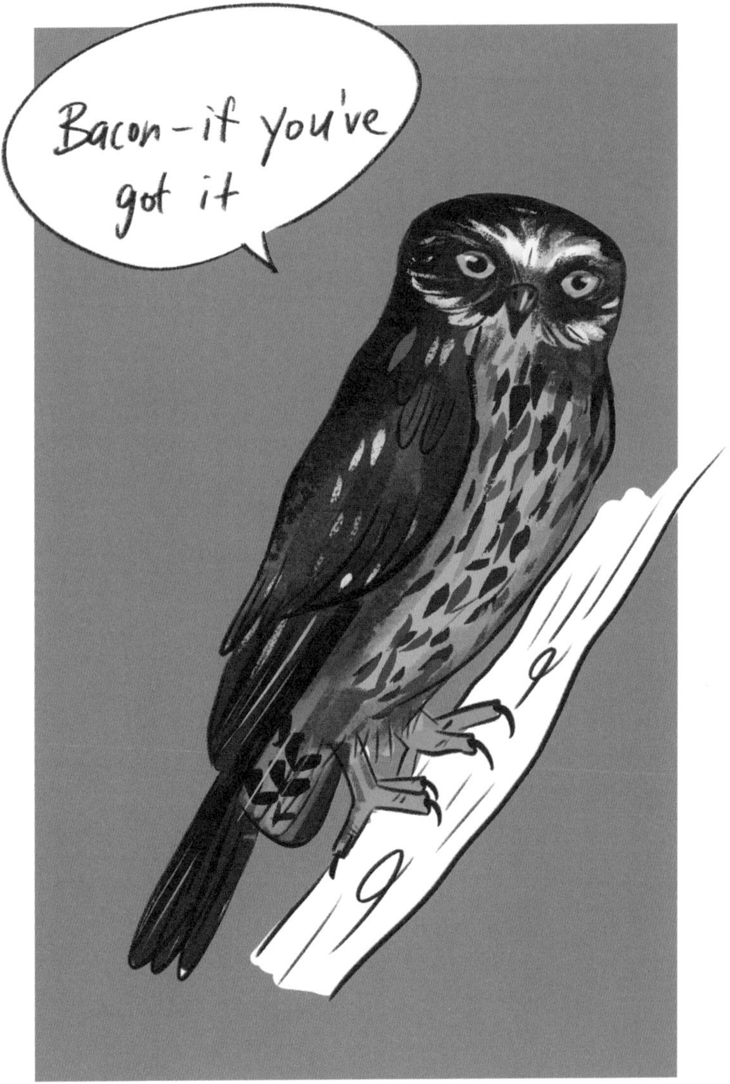
Bacon–if you've got it

If it sounds like the shower scene from *Psycho*...

it's the African gray hornbill. Living in sub-Saharan Africa with its namesake horned bill, the African gray hornbill may well remind you of a particular cartoon bird from a famous animated film about *Hamlet*. Okay, it was about lions and hyenas, but *Hamlet* all the same.

Speaking of famous movies, this bird's call echoes the soundtrack from the shower scene from *Psycho*. Which is ironic, since these birds live in the savanna and prefer open dry areas and woodlands. If it sounds like that noise that everyone makes when handling a knife and pretending to stab the food they are preparing—I mean, we all do that *ee-ee-ee* noise in that situation, right?—well, if you hear that and you're in say, Namibia, it might be an African gray hornbill.

If it sounds like haunting sleigh bells...

it's a bell miner. Making their home in Australia, bell miners live along the east coast of Queensland, New South Wales, and Victoria.

Their green feathers can make them hard to spot in the trees, so you may hear them before you see them. Known for their musical bell sounds, sometimes they can sound like jingle bells that you would find on Santa's sleigh, but more often the noise is that of achingly eerie silver bells—the bells worn by the ghosts of frail Victorian children.

If it sounds like you've got something stuck in your teeth...

it's a purple-backed fairywren. You're out at dinner and you've gotten something wedged next to your left incisor. The sucking sound you make with your tongue trying to get that piece of food out of your teeth (without resorting to using your fork as a toothpick) is the sound the purple-backed fairywren makes. And with that display, you're not getting a second date.

It's not a pleasant image for such an adorable, tiny, and colorful Australian bird. There are many fairywren species, all with a similar shape and vibe. Some are called splendid, some lovely, some superb, but the purple-backed has the largest range across the country and gives middle-child energy. You know, like when watching your parents introduce your siblings as lovely and splendid, and you get "well . . . they're purple."

Keep an eye and an ear out for these beauties when in Australia and maybe pack some dental floss.

If it sounds like a ghostly *oo-ooOo-ooOo* calling you in your dreams...

it's a white-browed coucal. This bird lives in sub-Saharan Africa and is part of the cuckoo family, but its song is not a sound you'd want chiming the hour. Well named for its expertly drawn white eyebrow, the coucal can be found clumsily banging about in brush along the eastern and central parts of the African continent. Or playing the ghost in a Scooby-Doo cartoon.

HA HA HA HA
HA HA HA HA HA
HA HA HA HA
HA HA HA HA
HA HA
HA
HA HA HA
HA HA HA
HA HA HA HA

If it sounds like that person who laughs a little too long at your jokes...

it's an Australian king parrot. Also known to make adorable squeaky chirps, the king parrot has a long, hyena-like laugh. Long, as in, a single call can last over 20 seconds. By the end of it, you just feel awkward standing there while they laugh at your, let's face it, medium-level joke at best.

Find these forest parrots with their green and red feathers all along the east coast of Australia.

If it sounds like a rusty swing slowly moving back and forth in a gentle breeze…

it's a korimako. Also known in its native New Zealand as the bellbird, its call suggests a hot, dry day when the sun is in full force and that small breeze isn't remotely enough to cool you down as you lie on the porch and drink lemonade. Or it's the reverse: a night scene in a scary movie as someone walks through a desolate playground with an ax as the swings sway on their own— it really depends on your mood.

Endemic to New Zealand, these honeyeaters feast on nectar and, like most New Zealand birds, are threatened by introduced mammals, including stoats, cats, and weasels. There's your scary movie— imagine your villain is a weasel.

We Owe Pigeons an Apology

Rats with wings. Vermin. Pests. We think of them as dirty city dwellers. We avoid them. We build elaborate mechanisms with spikes, nets, and other deterrents to keep them off our property . . . pigeons.

They are most likely the first domesticated bird in human history and have been used for millennia as a food source, as hobby birds, and to carry messages. Used in both World Wars to deliver the most vital of messages, several pigeons received medals and commendations for their service. All built with the most remarkable homing skills, pigeons find their way home over thousands of miles from places they've never seen before—but at some point, they fell out of fashion. Commonly connected with New York City and other large urban areas, pigeons originated in Europe and Asia but can now be found in cities spanning the globe.

Related to both the extinct passenger pigeon (whose numbers once reached the billions) and the dodo, more than 300 kinds of pigeons still live today all over the world. They sound like they are trying to coo but someone is holding their mouth shut. Known as domestic, feral, or rock pigeons, they are found mostly in cities because that's where humans are. And where humans are, food often is.

The dove—seen as clean, white, peaceful, and pure—belongs to the same family as pigeons. Doves have a much better publicist, it seems—you've never seen anyone release a dozen feral pigeons at their wedding, have you?

We taught the common pigeon to work with us humans, to like us, to love us—then we tossed them aside. Imagine if we chose one small, loyal, and trusting dog breed (poodles? Maltese? pugs?) and banished it to the streets, where we neglected and shunned it. That would be akin to what we have done to pigeons.

So the next time you walk by some pigeons spending time in a park or in your garden, maybe don't shoo them away so quickly. Tip your hat, give that closed-mouthed smile, and utter a small "Sorry" as you pass by.

8

Human Is as Human Does
Birds That Sound like Us

We humans like to think we are the greatest thing since avocado on toast, and we often project our own mannerisms and qualities onto the animal kingdom. We see faces in things that are not faces—like the man in the moon, or that wall outlet with a surprised expression. We equate bird sounds to human noises to make sense of them, to remember them, or because they make us giggle. Many birds really do sound like people laughing, like some species of woodpeckers, gulls, or ducks. Rest assured, they are laughing at us, not with us.

If it sounds like someone with a dry cough...

it's a dusky grouse. Picture it: You're in the theater—maybe it's a movie, maybe it's the ballet, maybe it's a one-woman show about the history of printer ink cartridges, I don't judge—but behind you and to the left is a person who can't stop clearing their throat. The kind of throat clearing that starts with a quiet *hem* and then turns into a loud series of back-of-the-throat coughs.

Now, if you are in the Rocky Mountains of Canada and the US, and your theater disrupter is a large brown bird with a reddish air sac on their neck, that sound could be a dusky grouse.

Not sure which is worse: the throat clearing or them leaning over to ask their companion repeated questions about the plot. "Who is that again? His brother? I thought he died."

If it sounds like sonar...

it's the resplendent quetzal. We need to use the word *resplendent* more. What a terrific word— I'd love to be referred to as resplendent. The resplendent quetzal is a brightly colored green, teal, and red bird with elegant tail feathers that are clearly there for impact—it really earns the title.

This national bird of Guatemala is featured on the country's flag, and it lives throughout Central America. It sounds like a submarine's sonar searching the dark waters with its low, repeating ping.

If it sounds like squeezing a rubber ducky...

it's a brown-headed nuthatch. These gravity-defying birds, like their red-breasted cousins, spend time in forests on trees hanging upside down. They live in the southeastern US, usually in pine forests, and can be found munching on insects.

Their grip strength must be off the charts to hold them in such positions, so don't challenge them to an arm-wrestling competition. They are only four inches long—you'd crush them—but they would take on the challenge as a matter of pride. Nonmigratory, they live year-round in the same place. As they are not great fliers, they spend time *in* the trees, but not soaring above them. Maybe someone shouldn't have skipped wing day.

If it sounds like a small child who is trying to get an adult's attention...

it's an ovenbird. These little brown birds repeat their two-tone call with each sound slightly louder than the one before. *Teacher teacher teacher teacher* they call while you are clearly in the middle of something, but kids—they're pretty cute, so we let them get away with it.

These warblers live in North and Central America in forests and are hard to spot, so listening for their yelling is the best way to find them.

If it sounds like a pedestrian crosswalk alert...

it's an eastern whip-poor-will. One of the nightjar family of birds, the eastern whip-poor-will looks like a log, with excellent bark camouflage for the forests that it calls home. It can be found, if you look hard enough, in eastern Canada and the US. They will migrate south into Mexico and Central America, but don't look for them west of Saskatchewan or Wyoming.

You might think their song sounds like their name—as if someone really has it out for Will and wants you to *whip poor WILL! Whip poor WILL!* Which is honestly a bit mean. But their song is much closer to the alert you hear on pedestrian crosswalks when it tells you it's safe to go. You should still check for cars, though—those drivers are menaces.

If it sounds like raucous laughter...

it's a kookaburra. King of the bush is he. Kookaburras live up to the song, and their energetic laughing is typically heard in the morning. Maybe they think it's funny that you have to get up to go to work. Part of the kingfisher family, kookaburras live in Australia and New Guinea, yet their distinctive call is often added to jungle soundtracks of films set thousands of miles from the birds' home.

The laughing kookaburra is the most well known, but there are a few varieties of this bird, including the blue-winged, spangled, shovel-billed, and rufous-bellied (that just means they have a red tummy). Because the laughing kookaburra mates for life, they recommend having a partner who finds your jokes funny.

If it sounds like it's yelling "*HELLO*" to you from a distance...

it's a peacock. Though peacock is their common name, they are officially referred to as peafowl, with the male peacock getting all the glamour, and the female called a peahen. Mostly just a big pheasant with a better wardrobe, the peacock originated in the forests of India and Sri Lanka. These days you're more likely to see them in zoos and on the estates of private landowners.

The tail of the peacock can be five feet long and displays behind them as they shake the iridescent feathers slightly, all part of their big moves to win a mate. Their call of *hello* can be heard across quite a distance, and some say it sounds like a person yelling for help or looking for their French friend Léon. Or maybe yelling *hello* to their French friend Léon who needs help. Should we go check on him?

If it sounds like someone crying...

it's the common potoo. This nocturnal bird of Central and South America looks most like a puppet that someone has forgotten in the woods. Similar to an owl but with a gaping frog mouth, the common potoo has brilliant barklike markings that allow it to blend into the trees during the day and, when perched on the end of a branch, to become a part of the tree itself.

When it's awake, you'll notice its large round yellow eyes, which when seemingly closed still have tiny slits so it can sneak a sly look around, watching for dangers or just being nosy. It makes the sound you might hear from an actor overacting during a scene when they need to cry. *Boo hoo hoo hoo,* they cry, while the rest of the cast onstage thinks, *Oh great, Eloise is in one of her moods again; this will be a long performance.*

If it sounds like someone singing "Chicago"...

it's a California quail. If it sounds like it's answering the question "Where do I get the best deep-dish pizza?", it's a California quail. Their distinct *chi-CA-go* song can make you think that this quail is confused, since it only lives on the West Coast from southern British Columbia to the Baja peninsula.

They are not the only ones confused—this small ground-dwelling bird with the excellent head plumage is quite often featured on Christmas decorations and mistaken for the token of affection in the song where someone gives their love a ridiculous number of both birds and human entertainers over the course of 12 days. For while the California quail has more flair, it is most definitely not a partridge.

If it sounds like someone yelling *"Bob WHITE"*...

it's a northern bobwhite. Another small bird with a loud call is the northern bobwhite. Whoever named them wasn't feeling super creative that day, as that is the exact whistle they make. They seem to have lost a friend named Bob White and are yelling that in a crowd. *Bob WHITE!* Paging *Bob WHITE!*

These birds live in the central and eastern states of the US, the very southern tip of Ontario, and into Mexico and the Caribbean, where, if you're lucky, you can find them foraging on the ground. You are more likely to hear them before you see them, as their call can travel quite a distance.

If it sounds like Indiana Jones cracking a whip...

it's the eastern whipbird. The "eastern" in their name refers to the east coast of Australia, where this native bird lives with spiky head feathers and a flash of white feathers on its neck, which only adds to its style. The call of the male is a classic whip crack, heard throughout the rain forests where it resides.

Much more of a heard-but-not-seen bird, their whip-crack sound is both their namesake and the best way to locate them. Listen for a long and quiet high-pitched whistle at first, and then flinch when you hear the crack. Oh, that's just me? I am rather jumpy.

Eggs: Every Bird Starts Somewhere

There are over 10,000 different species of birds in the world. As varied as they possibly can be in their size, nests, diet, and coloring, feathers, and beaks—they could not be more vast in scope—the one thing that all birds have in common is that they started as an egg.

Even the eggs, though, come in quite the spectrum. Ostrich eggs are the largest of any living bird, with the volume of two dozen chicken eggs inside and a terribly thick shell, compared to miniscule hummingbird eggs that are around the size of a single pea. When a full-grown hummingbird can be smaller than three inches, the eggs need to be pretty tiny to be in scale.

Unless you're a kiwi. Kiwis have the largest egg-to-bird ratio, with their eggs coming in about a fifth of the mother's size. Hold a kiwi egg in your hand and it will barely fit, even though the North Island kiwi that it came from was hardly larger than a football. If a human were to have a baby at a fifth of their average weight, that baby would be around 30 pounds! Where do we sign to opt out of that?

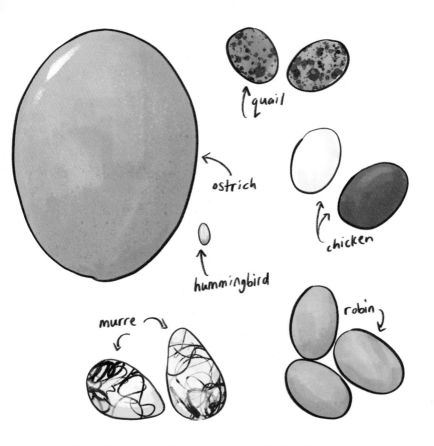

quail

ostrich

chicken

hummingbird

murre

robin

Even the eggs we know the best—chickens'—have great variety in color and size, and, no, the brown eggs aren't healthier than white eggs (it's not like bread). They get their color from the type of chicken.

Birds' eggs can be brilliantly colored (like robin's-egg blue), speckled for camouflage, or shaped so they don't roll off cliff tops. Eggs can be laid individually, with the emerging young raised as an only child, or in large clutches where almost everyone ends up with middle child syndrome.

9

Come Here Often?

Birds That Travel and Those That Don't

Some birds live their whole lives a few short miles from where they hatched. Some rack up more frequent-flier miles than a whole squad of flight attendants. Their desire to move, and where they go, seems out of their control. If they catch a bug in the air while migrating, is that an in-flight meal? And does it cost extra? At least there's no baggage fee.

If it sounds like someone catcalling with a whistle...

it's an upland sandpiper. These long-legged birds have charisma. Or at least confidence. Or at the very least, chutzpah. Their call sounds like they are giving you a wolf whistle or a catcall. A short, then long whistle that reminds you of a cartoon character with their eyes bugging out and love hearts floating around their heads.

Upland sandpipers like prairies and grasslands. They live in a pretty widespread area through all of North and South America and are a long-distance migrant, breeding in Canada and the US and wintering entirely in South America.

If it sounds like a chicken squawking…

it's a whooping crane. The tallest bird in North America, they stand at a height of about five feet with a tremendous seven-foot wingspan. Like other cranes, they prefer wetlands and marshes and live in small pockets in the eastern and southern US, with some populations migrating to spend their summers in Canada.

They mate for life, and sadly there are currently probably fewer than a thousand of these elegant birds. They are good fliers and can glide for some distance if they catch the wind right.

All that said, they sound like a cartoon chicken. Truly. Picture a cartoon on a farm with a lot of chickens walking around, and then someone walks by and startles them and they yell out *beck-KAH!* With a dash of trumpet for a bit of whimsy. That's the whooping crane.

If it sounds like a creaky rocking chair...

it's a sandhill crane. They can be found all over North America, from Alaska to Mexico, with permanent nesting spots in the Deep South in Florida, Georgia, and Mississippi, and in Cuba. They migrate to breed in Canada by the thousands. A social bird, they flock together in great quantities, and you can hear them from miles away.

At over four feet tall, these spindly-legged birds sound like a noisy wooden rocking chair being well used. Either the chair or the porch needs a good oiling. Like most cranes, they are happiest around waterways and marshy areas.

Their skill on the dance floor—in this case, wetlands—is well documented. They have an elaborate mating dance with spins, jumps, and lots of wing choreography. It must work, since they are one of the most abundant crane species.

If it sounds like someone slowly and aggressively ripping a thick piece of paper...

it's a snowy egret. Imagine tearing card stock, not tissue paper. The tearing is slow and deliberate, and you're ripping this paper while maintaining eye contact. It's a total power move. That's the sound. The snowy egret is quite stunning. So stunning, in fact, that they were nearly wiped out in the early 1900s due to the plume trade's high demand for their feathers.

They live in South and North America, preferring the coast and wetlands, where they use their thin black beaks to spear small fish for dinner.

If it sounds like
a dog chewing
a squeaky toy...

it's a northern flicker. These striking birds have a strong grasp of both color blocking and patterns. They live in the continental US and Canada. Dual passports can have a real payoff.

They sound just like a dog chewing furiously on a squeaky toy. You know the one—it's the toy you "lose" occasionally because your dog won't stop chewing it, and after an hour the sound makes you have a tiny breakdown. Pretty sure your dog still knows it's in that cupboard, though.

They are woodpeckers, so they do drum on trees with a very consistent and even rhythm, but you're more likely to spot them hanging out on the ground foraging down where they can find insects to eat without having to give themselves such a headache.

If it sounds like someone's playing *Wheel of Fortune...*

it's a yellow-bellied sapsucker. The woodpecker with the best name for yelling at someone as an insult in a black-and-white western is the yellow-bellied sapsucker—it's right up there with varmints, scallywags, and lily-livered horse thieves.

The part of the name we need to question here is "yellow-bellied," because these birds look like you colored their bellies in with a highlighter that had already run out of ink. At least they do actually suck sap, if that's any consolation, and would probably lose their damn minds if they ever tried maple syrup. They breed across Canada and the northeastern US and migrate down to the south, right into Central America.

Their drumming sounds like a spinning wooden prize wheel as it clicks past the marker and slows down. What will you win? A free spin? A coupon for a product you'll never use that you have to pick up in person at a store across town? A new car?!

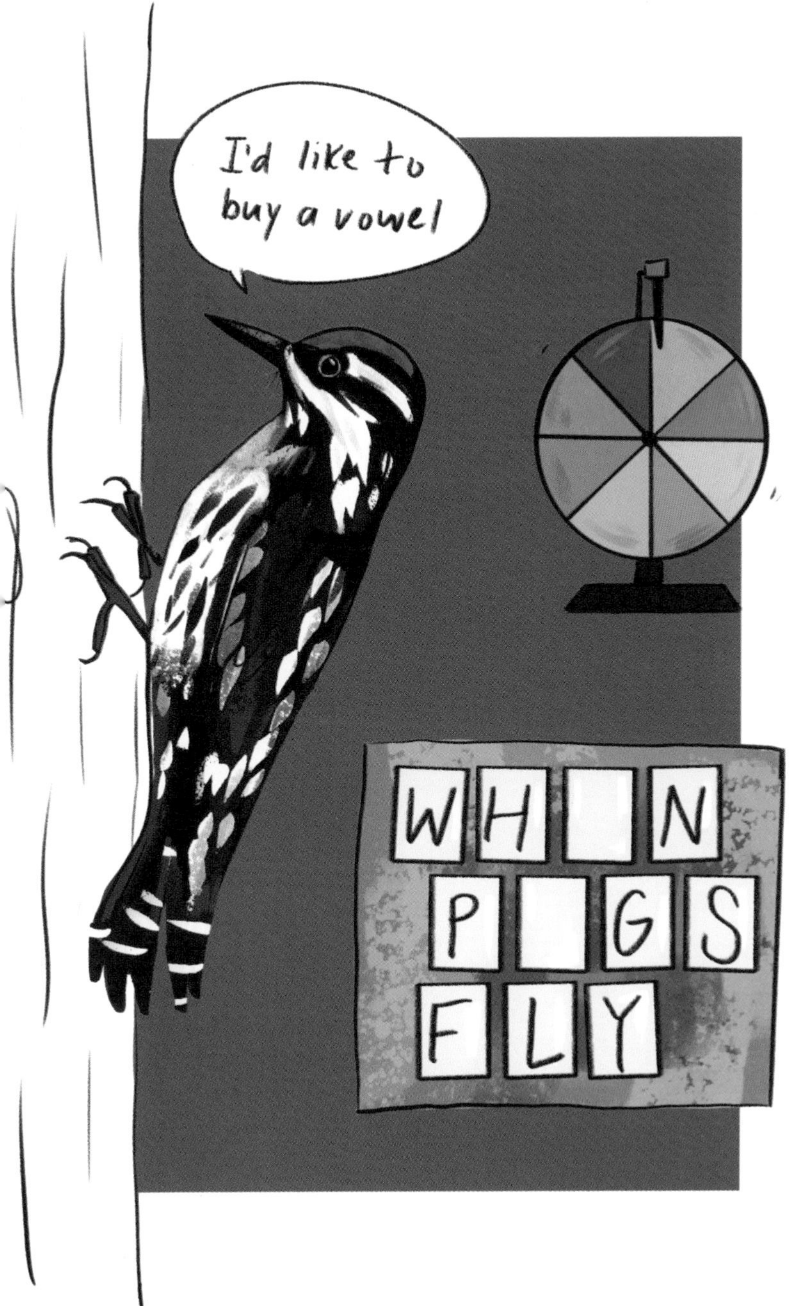
I'd like to buy a vowel
WH N
P GS
FLY

If it sounds like you are locking your car...

it's a gray flycatcher. That double *beep-boop* noise made as you press your fob while walking away from your car. Don't hit the other button: The alarm will go off, but not a single person will even for a second think that your car is being stolen; they'll all assume you sat on your keys again.

Living in the western US and down into Mexico, these little birds are mostly just mad at people for spelling their name *grey* instead of *gray*. They would also like you to know that it's not just flies that they eat—they like beetles and moths and grasshoppers. It's a well-rounded diet.

If it sounds like that squeaky shopping cart...

it's a killdeer. You're at the store, you have your reusable grocery bags, there's a list on your phone that you will completely forget to look at, and you've just grabbed a cart on your way in. Inevitably that cart will be the one with the wonky wheel that spins at a slower rate than the others and makes the cart squeal and drift left.

This plover lives all over North and Central America, and you can hear their high-pitched sound, which is also thought to sound like their name, *kill-deer*, though it's incredibly doubtful that these small birds have the strength for such a feat.

What they do have are performance skills. To get predators away from their nests, they put on a show with their broken wing routine that pulls focus from their eggs and young. So convincingly do they portray themselves as the easier target that they will have you throwing roses and screaming *Encore!*

If it sounds like a squeaky wagon wheel...

it's a comb-crested jacana. This long-legged bird is found in wetlands along the eastern and northern coast of Australia into Indonesia and neighboring islands, and it can be seen hanging out on lotus flowers and leaves so frequently that it's earned the nickname lotusbird. That loses points for imagination but gains a few for accuracy. They use their incredibly long feet to spread out their weight on the leaves, like snowshoes. With legs like that, it's unlikely they'd even get into the lotus position.

A dark brown bird with a white neck and belly, it sports a jaunty red comb, worn like a stylish beret or a fascinator by someone attending the Sunday races. Less elegant is the sound they make, that of a worn-out squeaky wagon wheel rolling along, in desperate need of some oiling. It's probably due to these birds spending so much time on the water—you know what that will do to metal.

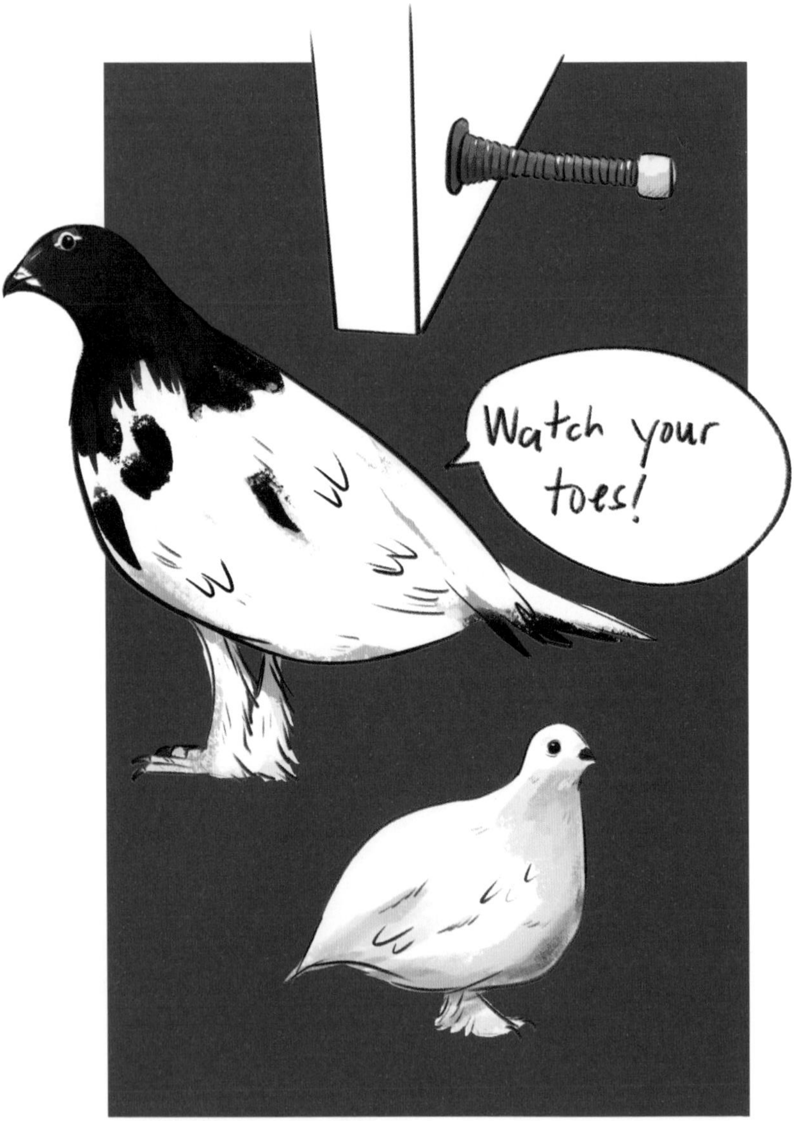
Watch your toes!

If it sounds like a doorstop spring...

it's a willow ptarmigan. First off, it's a silent *p*—like *pterodactyl*, *pneumonia*, or *receipt*. The willow ptarmigan is one of three different kinds of ptarmigans, all of which are a type of grouse. The others are the rock and the white-tailed. All of them live in tundra regions—they love the cold and don't migrate south, even living in the far north as they do.

This bird loves a costume change and switches feathers during the year, rocking all white in winter and sporting some brown and red feathers in summer to match the seasonal scenery. The willow ptarmigan sounds like you've just accidentally hit one of those springy doorstops on the back of the bathroom door.

Fun fact! The state bird of Alaska is the willow ptarmigan. Another fun fact! There's a town in Alaska called Chicken that wanted to name themselves after the ptarmigan but couldn't decide on the correct spelling. It was the 1800s; in their defense, they couldn't exactly have googled it.

CHICKEN
ALASKA
Population - 12

If it sounds like a muffled dirt bike motor...

it's an Atlantic puffin. The name Atlantic puffin implies the existence of a Pacific puffin, which does exist, but which is called the tufted puffin, which ruins the naming set but is terribly fun to say. On the West Coast of North America there is also the horned puffin, and it's important to note here that baby puffins are called pufflings. Because that's freaking adorable.

Back to the Atlantic puffin, a bird so named so it won't get lost. This small football-size bird lives in the North Atlantic sea eating fish or perching on rocky cliffs. The Atlantic puffin makes a sound like a dirt bike driving off in the distance. Maybe there's a motocross track near you, but you can only hear the muffled engines being revved. Maybe you're in Newfoundland on a desolate cliff, surrounded by small birds—could go either way.

Often confused with penguins, the two have never met in the wild. And if they did, the puffin would absolutely mock the penguin, for you see, puffins can fly!

If it sounds like a bird that smokes two packs a day...

it's a European starling. The European starling is an invasive species that lives all over North and Central America in the hundreds of millions and is the most prolific bird in North America. As the name suggests, they also live, and originated, in Europe, but they are found in parts of Asia, Australia, South America, and Africa, too. They form massive flocks called a murmuration, those mesmerizing forms of flying birds, both beautiful and ominous.

Their black feathers are dazzling in the sunlight, displaying a rainbow of colors. They seem to do everything in abundance, including their songs and calls, and make very passable imitations of other birds in their areas. When not mimicking, they can make droid-like short whistles, beeps, and clicks.

Often it seems like they want to sing a song but can't decide on which melody to choose, so they do them all at once. Their calls can be raspy and gravelly. If a sparrow or a lark has a sonorous singing voice, then a starling's call sounds like that bird with a 40-year heavy smoking habit.

If it sounds like wiggling a piece of aluminum siding in the air...

it's a Gunnison sage grouse. The Gunnison sage grouse is similar to a regular grouse, only with more herbs. Large brown-and-white birds that live in a super-select section of Colorado, the sage in the name isn't due to them being flavorful but to the sagebrush that they prefer to live in and eat. The males have two large chest sacs that they puff up with air when making their signature vocalization, which sounds like wobbling a thin piece of metal. Grab that piece of aluminum siding and give it a good shake: That's their mating noise, if that's what you're into.

The male sage grouse has a flair for fashion with a display of spiky tail feathers and the most elaborate collar of fluffy white feathers—and we are here for the drama.

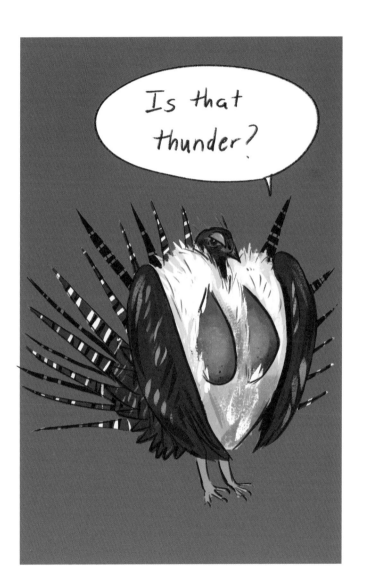

Migration: Should I Stay or Should I Go?

Not every part of the world has birds that migrate. Many birds live and stay in one place with no need to fly south to have their young or north to find food. Very different story in North America and Europe, where not only birds but people seasonally migrate. Those Canadian winters are no joke.

Some birds, like ducks or geese, can be seen on frozen lakes in winter (ice fishing, one assumes), and you'll observe and hear starlings, cardinals, chickadees, and others right through the snowy months. Cardinals didn't get that coveted Christmas card campaign by being out of town in December. They can stay because they have year-round food, they don't mind the cold, or they just don't have the energy to make the trip.

Other birds experience their first day with lowered temperatures and immediately get their passports stamped. The arctic tern has a name that suggests an appreciation for glaciers and blizzards, but this bird flies the farthest to get away from it all, traveling thousands of miles for a change of scenery, a different climate, and a bite to eat.

A white stork in the 1800s was found in Germany with a spear through its neck. The spear was made of wood that could only have come from the African continent. While this discovery was huge for learning about the migration of

birds, I think we glossed over the fact that the stork flew home with a damn spear stuck in it! Some people can't walk half a block with a pebble in their shoe.

Taking the same paths to the same places, often with hundreds or thousands of their closest friends, birds migrate and stop over at set points, like a hub airport but with less impact on the economy.

Migrating North American birds like the American robin, red-winged blackbirds, and bluebirds are far more indicative of spring's arrival than a groundhog that is fearful of its own shadow.

In contrast, practically all the grouse, prairie chicken, partridge, and pheasant family trees are entirely nonmigratory. Some people just really hate to unpack.

10

Cacophony, Commotion, and Clarity

Birds with Unique Sounds

Ah, the serenity of being alone with your thoughts on a crisp sunny day, the window slightly ajar as the curtains waft in the fragrant breeze, only to be made acutely aware of the volume, pitch, and otherworldly sounds coming from the birds outside. Eerie, alarming, or simply noisy, birds are masters at getting the attention of one another, and of us.

If it sounds like a ghostly wail...

it's a common loon. This bird is a Canadian icon. Canada's one-dollar coin with an image of the loon is most affectionately called a loonie. This is different from calling someone "looney," which as you know is a bit unkind and derives from the word *lunatic*. Though one of the collective nouns for a group of loons is asylum, which really does not help matters much.

The common loon is almost exclusively seen on water and needs expanse of it as a runway to wind up for takeoff. Since they are mostly viewed from a distance, people think loons are smaller than they really are, but these birds can be three feet long. They live across Canada and along the coast of North America.

While nostalgic for some, the sound of a common loon is an eerie and creepy soundtrack to any thriller film. They yodel, they hoot, and they wail like a wolf howling at the moon. If you were alone at night by a lake in a remote part of Canada and heard that, the hairs on the back of your neck would stand up. Also, why are you alone in the woods at night? That's, like, really unsafe.

If it sounds like
an owl hooting...

it's a mourning dove. If you thought a loon call was nostalgic, then the mourning dove would like to enter the chat. They are named mourning doves because their song sounds so woeful and mournful. I reckon a lot of you reading this right now are immediately surprised that it is not a morning dove, like there is also somewhere an afternoon and evening dove.

Making their home from Canada down to the Panama Canal, these doves can be found in a multitude of habitats, from rural areas to cities, and more specifically the ledge right outside my window. Their melancholic song sounds like sighing and is very similar to the hoots of an owl. So much so that, given their wide distribution, there is an extremely good chance that the "owls" you've been hearing are, in fact, mourning doves. As we've discovered already in this book, most owls don't have that typical *who-who-who* sound. The clincher is if you hear the bird fly away. Mourning doves have a distinctive and loud flutter as they fly. Owls are as silent as the grave.

If it sounds like someone absentmindedly tapping their pencil on the table...

it's a yellow rail. These tiny, squat brown birds are notoriously hard to spot, so listening for them is a good way to find them. And look down, as they hang out on the ground in marshy areas. When you can find them, they will be in Canada and the US.

Oh, and bring a flashlight. They mostly make the pencil-tapping sound at night. Then again, a bird trying this hard to not be found—that's a good clue that they are just not that into you.

If it sounds like an alien trying to talk to you in their language…

it's an Australian magpie. These birds look like a crow that has rolled around in some white paint, but they are not related directly to crows, ravens, or even magpies. They got their name based on their resemblance to the European version, but only in looks.

These birds are known for their incredible array of songs and noises, from mimicking other birds and animals to the otherworldly warbling flutelike songs that, once you've heard them, you will henceforth notice in the background of your favorite Australian TV shows.

Those more personally familiar with these birds, who live in Australia and New Zealand, are well acquainted with swooping season, which happens during spring. Stray too close to their nests, and you'll be met with an air assault. They like to raise their young in gardens, playing fields, and parks, and it turns out humans like to spend time there as well. Keep calm and carry an umbrella.

If it sounds like space lasers being fired in a battle...

it's a purple martin. Or maybe it's your 12th birthday party and you and your friends are smashing it up on the laser tag course. These birds are decidedly more blue than purple and were probably named by the same person who named the blueberry, the red panda, cheesecake, or Chilean sea bass. Goodness, we have a lot of things with inaccurate names.

The largest of the North American swallows, they breed in eastern North America and migrate to South America. They prefer ponds, lakes, and open areas and have a unique talent for getting almost all their food from the air while flying. Gosh, they would absolutely go crazy for a drive-through.

If it sounds like a whole bunch of car alarms going off…

it's a rock wren. The rock wren, a tiny brown-and-gray bird, is hard to spot, as its coloring allows it to blend in with the desert and rocky canyon settings of western North America that they prefer. Thankfully they found a way for you to recognize them, and it's by having a song that sounds like every car alarm in a parking lot going off at once.

It's that scene from an action film after a sonic boom from a building exploding, the aftermath of an earthquake, or maybe just the parking lot outside a golf course after a rogue golf ball bounces through. Each rock wren song contains at least three variations of car alarm noises, changing pitch and frequency but consistent in their short, staccato bursts.

If it sounds like
a weed whacker...

it's a rhinoceros auklet. Related to puffins, the seabird with the best name is the rhinoceros auklet. Already it sounds like something jewel-covered and cursed that treasure hunters would search for on wild adventures. The rhinoceros auklet lives along the Pacific coast from Mexico up to Alaska and across the ocean to Japan and down to Korea. The tiny horn on the top of their bill is where they get their name, and recently scientists have found that it has fluorescent qualities so other rhinoceros auklets can see it, like a beacon, at night and underwater when ultraviolet spectrums are enhanced.

These birds sound like weed whackers, those high-pitched, whining string trimmers that edge lawns no one is allowed to walk on. It must be in some landscape maintenance handbook that these power tools work only on weekend mornings before 9 a.m. You'd prefer a colony of auklets if you had the choice, even if they do smell like fish.

If it sounds like an expert whistler...

it's a white-throated sparrow. These small songbirds live in Canada and the US and have the most melodic whistle, with perfect pitch, and can hold that note in their songs like a classically trained whistler. There have to be classically trained whistlers, right?

Living in forests and wooded areas and being mostly brown, these sparrows are hard to spot, so you'll likely hear them before catching a glimpse. Males have a splash of highlighter yellow above their eye, because everyone needs a little pop of color sometimes.

If it sounds like a robot trying to communicate…

it's a bobolink. The bobolink has a name that sounds like it's from a science fiction line of dialogue: "Once we connect the bobolink to the hyperspatial underdrive, we can go to superluminal speed and hide from the B5-R7 battalion." A name that matches well with this bird that sounds like our companion droid in that scene. Without even the luxury of subtitles, who knows what those little robots are beeping on about—they could be swearing up a storm!

Migrating from Canada to South America, the males of this black-and-white bird species look like they are wearing a small blond wig. You can spot them in grasslands, meadows, and fields. Listen for their mechanical chattering beeps, buzzes, and clicks, and hope they are not saying anything mean about you.

If it sounds like someone is cleaning plastic...

it's a Swainson's thrush. You made too much marinara sauce and put the leftovers in a plastic container in the fridge and then later consumed the delicious sauce on some pasta. Now you are scrubbing this container in the sink within an inch of its life trying to get that red stain out. That sound you're making while desperately scrubbing the plastic, working faster with each wipe as you contemplate just throwing the container out, is the sound of a Swainson's thrush.

Breeding in Canada and migrating to South America for winter, these birds blend so well into their forest dwellings that listening for their Tupperware-scrubbing sound may be an easier way to find them than trying to catch a glimpse. And while you're looking for them, maybe think about getting some glass food containers.

If it sounds like the loudest bird you've ever heard...

it's a white bellbird. The loudest bird in the world is the South American white bellbird. We all have a friend who talks at a louder-than-normal volume (or maybe you are that friend), but that person has nothing on the white bellbird. Clocking in at around 125 decibels (somewhere between a chain saw and your average rock concert), this bird sounds like the national emergency alert on your phone, if your phone were 100 phones at once. To add to their charm, they have a long wattle that extends from their beaks, which evokes a 1990s rat-tail hairstyle.

You would think that the purpose of their volume would be to carry a message across great distances, yet instead the male white bellbirds yell it into the face of their intended as a gesture of love and a display of their vocal stylings. It's no declaration of love in a handwritten sonnet, but it does work as a grand gesture, if being screamed at directly into your face is what you're into.

If it sounds like someone shuffling through their playlist...

it's a northern mockingbird. This average-size gray bird isn't much to look at, but they make up for that in personality. The northern mockingbird lives across the US, Mexico, and southern parts of Canada. They live near humans in towns and cities, and you can spy them in your backyard, in parks, and in farmers' fields.

If it sounds like every bird in this book is outside your window singing up a storm, it might be a single northern mockingbird. *Single* being the key word here, as the male mockingbird shuffles through his entire playlist trying to find the right genre to impress during mating season. Some of the greatest impressionists of the bird world, the mockingbird can imitate numerous other birds' songs and calls and often does multiple sounds in one song. If the sound of a blue jay doesn't please his intended, he can try a bluebird, a sparrow, a cardinal, or others until he finds the right combination to woo her.

Can You Keep It Down? Loud Birds

Birds make noise. It's one of their most noted characteristics and one of the few things shared across the thousands of species of birds we have on Earth. Some birds are quite quiet, making only a peep, barely a sound—but even the mute swan isn't mute. Everyone needs some way to communicate, and birds never really got into texting.

Then there are birds that have you rushing for your noise-canceling headphones. Birds that live in metropolitan areas need to be loud, if only to get their sounds heard over the din of humanity. From the red-winged blackbird that sounds like a fax machine or old-school dial-up internet, to the red-headed woodpecker that mixes its drumrolls with screaming calls just to make sure you're up, birds are skilled at making their presence known. Maybe the red on these birds is a warning label.

Birds need to make noise for a multitude of reasons: announcing that they've found food or yelling "Look behind you!" They can also sing and chirp and screech to mark their territory for any intruders, be it friend or foe. Male birds sing loudly as their way of flirting, and some of you know what it's like to be serenaded in public, so you know that can go either way.

As seen throughout this book, birds can and do make an expansive array of noises. They whistle (both well and

246

red-headed woodpecker

red-winged blackbird

mute swan

not so well), they gulp, they hiss, they scream. The white bellbird is the current champion in terms of decibels, but many birds can produce sounds at a staggering volume, and they seem to enjoy doing that in the mornings. The dawn chorus as they greet the day isn't always timed to your schedule. But neither is that neighbor who thinks that a leaf blower is fair use at 8 a.m. on a Sunday.

Truthfully, we don't know all the reasons why birds sing—as with any language that you don't speak or understand, it can be hard to find the nuances and reasons. Maybe sometimes they just like the sound of their own voice. Maybe sometimes we like it, too.

Now, will you please keep it down? I need a nap.

Resources

BirdLife Australia
birdlife.org.au

Britannica
britannica.com
/Animals-Nature

**Cornell Lab of Ornithology:
All About Birds**
allaboutbirds.org/news

**Cornell Lab of Ornithology:
eBird**
ebird.org/home

Ducks Unlimited Canada
ducks.ca

National Audubon Society
audubon.org

New Zealand Birds Online
nzbirdsonline.org.nz

**New Zealand Department
of Conservation**
doc.govt.nz

**The Royal Society for the
Protection of Birds**
rspb.org.uk

Acknowledgments

I'd like to thank my editor, Kristen Hewitt, and the team at Storey Publishing for all their support and encouragement; I am in your debt. My family and friends have had to listen to me talk about birds for far too much of their lives and I will love you forever for it. To everyone online who has watched, liked, shared, and left such lovely comments on my posts—you're swell. Thanks for the joy you've brought me.